EXAMINATION OF THE CHILD
WITH
MINOR NEUROLOGICAL DYSFUNCTION

Clinics in Developmental Medicine No. 71

Examination of the Child
with
Minor Neurological Dysfunction

SECOND EDITION

BERT C. L. TOUWEN

Preface by
MARTIN BAX

1979
Spastics International Medical Publications
LONDON: William Heinemann Medical Books
PHILADELPHIA: J. B. Lippincott Co.

SBN 0 433 32622 0

First published 1970

Printed in England at THE LAVENHAM PRESS LTD., Lavenham, Suffolk

Contents

Preface

The need for a standardised examination of the neurological system of the child has grown rather than diminished since the first edition of this book was published in 1970. The validity of the examination proposed by the author, confirmed not only by the steady sale of the book over the years since publication but by the fact that in preparing this new edition—apart from many refinements and modifications of the techniques described—the actual form of the examination has not been changed from that described in the original edition. Workers familiar with the original tool will therefore welcome this old friend, which now incorporates the modifications resulting from seven years' experience of the instrument.

The demand for such a book has increased, not because clinicians are seeing more children with overt neurological diseases, but because in the intervening years the interest in the possible relationship between behaviour displayed by the young child and the organ responsible for producing this behaviour—the brain—has increased. Paediatricians and paediatric neurologists are called upon more and more to examine children presenting with behavioural and learning problems to see whether there is any evidence that such children are neurologically disturbed. In new and expanded chapters the author discusses the difficulties and dangers inherent in some of the assumptions which underlie the referral of such children to a doctor. The new chapter on the neurological examination and minimal brain dysfunction, and the author's final discussion on the relationship between minor neurological dysfunction and behaviour, by themselves make this a vital addition to all clinicians' shelves, and such discussion emphasises again the need for a reliable tool with which to examine the child.

In welcoming this second edition I can therefore do no better than to repeat the same comments that I wrote in 1970 in welcoming the first edition: "The first need in studying these children is the development of a reliable tool. Those familiar with the studies which Prechtl and his co-workers have made on babies will recognise in this book the same meticulous attention to detail that characterised their previous work." (It must be emphasised how Touwen is following in this tradition.) "Each test is clearly described and illustrated and a proforma allows the results to be recorded in a manner which is readily quantifiable. With this tool, the physician is equipped to study the child with minor neurological dysfunction, in addition to assessing reliably those with major dysfunction."

MARTIN BAX

CHAPTER 1

Introduction

The designing of a specific and rather extensive neurological examination for children, with a view to the detection of minor deviations in their neural functions, requires some justification. Why are the usual neurological techniques employed by many neuropaediatricians and neurologists insufficient? This question can be divided into two sub-questions: why a specific examination for children, and why an examination for minor deviations?

The answer to the first sub-question is that the child's nervous system is qualitatively different from that of an adult. It is a rapidly developing nervous system, while the adult's has reached a relatively stable phase of development. Consequently the examination technique has to take into account the developmental changes in nervous output which occur throughout childhood. This implies that the examiner must be familiar with the natural history of the neurological repertoire, because some neurological phenomena will merely change with age (*e.g.* diadochokinesis), while others disappear altogether (*e.g.* many associated movements). Moreover, there are several neurological signs which are specific to childhood. For example choreiform dyskinesia, if present, is usually more prominent during childhood than in adulthood, and minor deviations of gait can be observed more easily during childhood than at a later age when walking is fully differentiated. It is clear, therefore, that an examination technique based on adult neurological functions is inadequate for use with children because the examiner cannot evaluate the specific properties of the developing nervous system. The method used must be a *developmental* neurological examination.

The answer to the second sub-question—why an examination for minor deviations?—is related to the indication for the neurological examination. Generally speaking, there are three main groups of indications for which children must be examined neurologically, with special emphasis on minor deviations. First, there is the suspicion of a neurological disease in its initial stage, on the basis of the history of the child's complaints (*e.g.* headaches and vomiting, or slow deterioration of mental and/or motor abilities) or on the familial history (*e.g.* tuberous sclerosis or muscle disease). Secondly, there are children with an obvious neurological disorder, for example some form of cerebral palsy, for whom it is important to discover all those facets of their neurological condition which are significant in deciding on treatment. For example, a child with overt hemiplegia may be found to have minor co-ordination difficulties in the 'normal' hand which require treatment. In both instances the examination technique must be refined enough to enable the examiner to detect slight neurological dysfunction.

Thirdly, many children are referred for a full neurological examination because of complaints by parents or teachers about behavioural and/or learning difficulties which have no apparent neurological cause, and who have no other disorder which would offer an obvious neurological clue. It is this third category of children with which this book is mainly concerned. The purpose is to assist the examiner who is asked about the possibility of neurological dysfunction which could be considered a so-called 'organic base' for the aberrant behaviour. The neurological dysfunction, if present, will be minor, so the examination must be detailed and comprehensive in order to scrutinize a large variety of neural mechanisms.

It is essential to have a clear idea of what a neurological examination will reveal. Learning and behavioural problems are only part of complex patterns of behaviour, defined as the whole set of actions carried out by the child with the purpose of changing his environment, or himself in relation to that environment. Of course, complex behaviour is mediated by the nervous system, but the neurological examination, which by its very nature must be limited, can assess only the part of this behaviour which falls within the scope of the examination itself (*e.g.* sensorimotor function, posture and motility, reactions and responses). The absence of minor neurological signs is no proof of the perfect integrity of the brain, nor does their presence automatically imply a causal relationship with the manifested behaviour; this may be so in some cases—for example clumsy motility in a child with slight co-ordination defects or choreiform dyskinesia—but is certainly not so in all cases. This point is discussed in Chapters 2 and 13; here it will suffice to say that a child with behavioural and learning difficulties should be assessed neurologically because the brain is involved in generating his behaviour and the neurological assessment enables the examiner to evaluate at least part of the integrity of the brain. The assessment may not result in a specific diagnosis of the cause of the behavioural disorder, but it must still be considered a necessary part of the diagnostic process.

Obviously the neurological examination should detect functional defects or substantiate their absence, but it should also differentiate these defects from deviations which stem from a lag in the speed of maturation of the brain (*i.e.* signs of neurological retardation), which is not necessarily the result of brain damage. The aim of a refined and age-appropriate examination technique is to differentiate these cases. It is important, too, to emphasize the difference between a neurological examination and a developmental assessment. The latter is mainly concerned with correct performances in accordance with the maturational timetable for any particular behaviour. The neurological examination, in contrast, is concerned with the way in which the child performs the task, the developmental changes of the performance being taken into account (see also Touwen 1974).

The neurological assessment described in this book is part of the methodological arsenal of a new specialization. As it concerns the most complex system of the organism, it is not surprising that it involves equally complex methods of examination which may appear difficult and time-consuming, requiring special skills and knowledge. However, it is impossible to design a series of 'crucial' neurological tests which will indicate whether the brain is functioning normally or abnormally. A plea for a short form of neurological screening for this purpose, though understandable, ignores essential properties of the central nervous system. A test of one single part of the neurological repertoire, for example grasping or walking, may give information about that particular function but it will not evaluate the neurological mechanisms on which the function is based, and such evaluation is necessary in the case of inadequate performance. Moreover, the examination of a single aspect of the nervous system—co-ordination for example—does not give sufficient information about other aspects such as muscle power or reflexes.

It is self-evident that functions such as hearing, speech and vision must also be assessed carefully at a level of speciality which falls outside the scope of this book. These should be done separately from the neurological assessment as the combination of assessments would take too much time and would be too fatiguing for the child, giving unreliable results. This book deals only with the routine neurological assessment, so no special attention is paid to the particular assessment of these other functions. For the same reason, electroencephalographic examinations will not be discussed.

A final remark must be made on the problem of so-called 'normative values'. In Groningen we have been following up for many years groups of babies who underwent very careful examinations in the neonatal period, and we have been developing techniques for assessing their later neurological performance. This book discusses the optimal tool, so far as we have been able to design it, for carrying out the neurological assessment of children between three and twelve years of age. We describe what we have found to be the normal developmental course and the normal performance of healthy children in this age-range in the specific population we have studied. In the course of our work, and with increasing experience, we have found cause to question the value of general 'population norms'. We feel that populations vary so much—for example children living in large towns compared with those living in small villages or rural areas; children of different socio-economic or ethnic backgrounds; children of different sexes—that 'absolute' norms can hardly ever be achieved. Every examiner has to try to find his own norms for his own population for many of the items in this neurological assessment in order to be able to interpret his findings reliably. The purpose of this book is to offer a standardized and comprehensive method for the neurological examination of children which should enable the examiner to relate his own findings with those from other sources, and so to gain insight into his patients' problems.

CHAPTER 2

The Neurological Examination and MBD*

Since Goldstein (1936) and Strauss and Werner (1943) assumed the existence of a syndrome of cerebral dysfunction which manifested itself both in the neurological and behavioural dimensions, many authors have tried to differentiate this 'syndrome' into clearly recognisable entities. Others have criticized this differentiation and, indeed, the whole concept of a such a syndrome. Discussion on the issue is far from finished and a list of relevant articles is given at the end of this chapter. But one cannot fail to conclude that the exclamation "It is time this idea of a syndrome was scotched before it gets too firmly entrenched in the literature" (Pond 1960) has been uttered in vain. Unfortunately, such a syndrome is prevalent in the neuropaediatric and psychological literature of the last two decades.

The issue with which we are concerned here is the presumed relationship between behavioural disorders and neurological dysfunction in children. This relationship presupposes a well-defined set of behavioural and learning disorders on the one hand, and well-defined neurological dysfunction on the other. However, the difficulties of definition have already been illustrated by Walzer and Richmond (1973), among others (Table I), and Becker (1976), who lists more than 50 symptoms, but adds innocently: "Interestingly, some children with MBD may be behaviourally quite different". In this quotation MBD stands for 'Minimal (or Minor) Brain Dysfunction (or Damage)'. However, it is essential to distinguish between neurological dysfunction and a behavioural aspect of this so-called syndrome if the assumed relationship between neurological dysfunction and behavioural disorder is to be studied.

In general, three approaches to this issue can be distinguished. In the first place one may start with children with brain damage and see whether they show clearly different behaviour from that of children without brain damage. This approach was adopted by Eisenberg (1957), Shaffer *et al.* (1974) and Rutter (1977), who use distinct and indisputable neurological conditions as criteria for brain damage, ranging from epilepsy and cerebral palsy to depressed skull fractures with gross damage to the brain. Of course, the heterogeneous character of the brain damage has to be taken into account when considering the results of the studies. The studies of Wolff and Hurwitz (1973) and Stine *et al.* (1975), among others, are examples of the same type of approach, but they use the presence of minor neurological signs as an indication of neurological dysfunction. The results of all these studies suggest that relationships between neurological dysfunction and behavioural disorders are variable and are strongly influenced by factors such as intelligence, social class, home environment and so on.

The second approach is based on a classification of children according to the

---

*Variously defined as minimal (or minor) brain dysfunction (or damage).

4

TABLE I

Some of the labels applied to learning and behavioural disorders (Walzer and Richmond 1973)

Minimal brain damage
Minimal cerebral dysfunction
Clumsy child syndrome
Visual-motor disability
Hyperkinetic syndrome
Dyslexia
Specific reading disability
Congenital word blindness
Perceptual motor handicaps
Production or acquisition learning problem
Strepho symbolia

presence or absence of behavioural and learning difficulties, accompanied by a search for evidence of neurological dysfunction. Examples of this are the studies of Werry (1968), Satterfield *et al.* (1972), O'Malley and Eisenberg (1973), Stephenson (1975), Steinhausen (1976) and McMahon *et al.* (1977), who took hyperactivity as their target symptom of behavioural difficulties; Schain (1972), Adams *et al.* (1974) and Hart *et al.* (1974), who used learning disabilities and under-achievement at school as a criterion; Rutter and Yule (1975), who studied reading retardation, and Shaffer *et al.* (1974), who measured 'conduct disorder' using a questionnaire filled in by the mothers. The relationship between the behavioural disorder and neurological dysfunction in these studies was not straightforward; again, the absence or presence of other variables played an important rôle.

The third approach is represented by those studies which are based on the concept of MBD as a clinical entity caused by cerebral dysfunction, and which focus on the aetiology of the condition. The subjective use of the terms MBD (which may or may not cover all the behavioural and learning difficulties) and cerebral dysfunction (which may or may not include neurological dysfunction) confuse the issue (*e.g.* Sainz 1966, Paine 1968, Wender 1971, Satz *et al.* 1971, Mangold 1974, Arnold 1976). One gets the impression that authors who take this approach consider the problem of the brain-behaviour relationship to be solved.

The variability in clinical symptomatology remains the crucial point and might be explained by differences in the degree of cerebral impairment (by biochemical disturbance or maturational lag for example), but other factors such as environment, basic intelligence and so on obviously also play a rôle. However, the matter is not as simple as that. When we say that 'behaviour' is mediated by the brain, this does not mean that 'normal' (acceptable) behaviour implies a 'normal' (intact) brain, or that disturbed behaviour (for example, behaviour that is labelled as MBD behaviour) implies an abnormal brain (one that is damaged for instance). 'Abnormal' brains can generate socially acceptable behaviour, as is demonstrated by epileptics, or by the fact that children without behavioural or learning difficulties may show various types of minor neurological dysfunction. On the other hand, 'normal' brains may generate a wide variety of behaviour when tested under extreme conditions. As will be discussed further in Chapter 13, any actual type of behaviour depends on the natural history of the brain under consideration, and many variables, endogenous and exogenous, play a part in this history. One may contend, therefore, that no two brains are completely similar, just as no two behaviours are completely similar. When one realises that the neurological examination merely evaluates one part of the brain, one is hardly surprised by Gomez' remark (1967): "Minimal cerebral dysfunction (maximal neurologic confusion)".

In searching for brain-behaviour relationships the aim should be to analyse the way in which the brain is able to cope with the demands of the environment, while considering the variability of the brain and the variability of the environment. Consequently, an accurate and objective description of the disorder is needed in the case of children with behavioural and learning difficulties. This is necessary both from a neurological and a behavioural point of view (Barlow 1974, Stephenson 1975, Yule 1978), while environmental influences have also to be considered at the same time (Sameroff and Chandler 1975). Moreover, it is important to take into account the interrelationships of the different methods applied to obtain a measurement (or result). Because of this, it is advisable to use a wide range of methods to ensure that the relationships found are really trait-relationships, and need not be attributed to method variance (see Hopkins 1976).

An example of this type of approach is Kalverboer's study of neurobehavioural relationships in pre-school children (1975). In this carefully designed study the relationships were found to be dependent on the situation in which the behaviour was observed. Moreover, boys and girls showed different relationships between the behaviour and the neurological condition. For instance, girls with unfavourable neurological scores tended to show a high degree of room exploration when alone with the mother, while girls with more favourable scores showed a considerable amount of discomfort. Such evident difference was not found in the boys, however, in whom unfavourable neurological scores appeared to be related to a low level of play activity in a situation where there was a small variety of toys, while the same boys showed a relatively high level of play activity when a great variety of toys was available. In the boys, the various categories of neurological make-up which were distinguished (sensorimotor, posture, co-ordination, choreiform dyskinesia, maturation of functions or responses, for example) also showed different relationships with behavioural variables from the girls. But Kalverboer has emphasised the point that only to a very limited degree (4 to 8 per cent) can the variance of his results be explained by neurobehavioural relationships, a warning which should be kept in mind when reading about these relationships between, for example, learning disorders and neurological signs (Adams *et al.* 1974, Hart *et al.* 1974, Stine *et al.* 1975), distractibility of performance and 'brain damage' (Schulman *et al.* 1965), reading difficulties and choreiform dyskinesia (Wolff and Hurwitz 1973), or between perinatal conditions and behaviour at pre-school or school age (Werry 1968), to mention only a few. One should never forget that these are statistical relationships which account for only a limited part of the variance in the patient material, so that individual predictions can hardly ever be made (Barlow 1974).

The present technique for the neurological examination of children, with its

6

special emphasis on minor neurological abnormalities, offers an instrument which enables the examiner to make a refined appraisal of the neurological make-up in cases where a traditional diagnosis is not feasible. It is a suitable technique for the neurological part of the diagnostic procedure of a child with behavioural and learning disorders, which may be important for treatment of the particular child, since treatment of a mild neurological disorder may influence general behaviour favourably. At the same time it is a prerequisite for the study of neurobehavioural relationships.

SOME CRITICAL COMMENTS ON THE MBD CONCEPT

Pond, D. (1960) 'Is there a syndrome of brain damage in children?' *Cerebral Palsy Bulletin,* **2,** 296-297.
Bax, M., Mac Keith, R. (1963) *Minimal Cerebral Dysfunction. Clinics in Developmental Medicine, No. 10.* London: Spastics Society with Heinemann.
Birch, H. G. (1964) *Brain Damage in Children.* Baltimore: Williams & Wilkins.
—— Thomas, A., Chess, S. (1964) 'Behavioral development in brain damaged children.' *Archives of General Psychiatry,* **11,** 596-603.
Schulman, J. L., Kaspar, J. C., Throne, F. M. (1965) *Brain Damage and Behavior.* Springfield, Ill.: C. C. Thomas.
Gomez, M. R. (1967) 'Minimal cerebral dysfunction (maximal neurologic confusion).' *Clinical Pediatrics,* **6,** 589-591.
Werry, J. S. (1968) 'Studies on the hyperactive child. IV. An empirical analysis of the minimal brain dysfunction syndrome.' *Archives of General Psychiatry,* **19,** 9-16.
Schain, R. J. (1972) *Neurology of Childhood Learning Disorders.* Baltimore: Williams & Wilkins.
Arnold, L. E. (1973) 'Is this label necessary?' *Journal of School Health,* **43,** 510-514.
Walzer, S., Richmond, J. B. (1973) 'The epidemiology of learning disorders.' *Pediatric Clinics of North America,* **20,** 549-565.
—— Wolff, P. H. (Eds.) (1973) 'Minimal cerebral dysfunction in children.' *Seminars in Psychiatry,* **5,** (1).
Barlow, C. F. (1974) '"Soft signs" in children with learning disorders.' *American Journal of Diseases of Children,* **128,** 605-606.
Stephenson, P. S. (1975) 'The hyperkinetic syndrome: some misleading assumptions.' *Canadian Medical Association Journal,* **113,** 764, 767-769.
Gellis, S. S. (1975) 'Editorial comment.' *American Journal of Diseases of Children,* **129,** 1324.
Kalverboer, A. F. (1975) *A Neurobehavioural Study in Pre-school Children. Clinics in Developmental Medicine, No. 54.* London: S.I.M.P. with Heinemann.
—— (1978) 'MBD: discussion of the concept.' *Advances in Biological Psychiatry,* **1,** 5-17.
Rutter, M. (1977) 'Brain damage syndromes in childhood: concepts and findings.' *Journal of Child Psychology and Psychiatry,* **18,** 1-21.
Shaffer, D. (1978) 'Natural history of the minimal brain dysfunction syndrome.' *Advances in Biological Psychiatry,* **1,** 18-34.
Touwen, B. C. L. (1978) 'Minimal brain dysfunction and minor neurological dysfunction.' *Advances in Biological Psychiatry,* **1,** 55-67.
Yule, W. (1978) 'Developmental psychological assessment.' *Advances in Biological Psychiatry,* **1,** 35-54.

CHAPTER 3

The Design of a Neurological Examination Technique for the Detection of Minor Neurological Signs

A neurological examination should be a comprehensive assessment of neural functions and should therefore be as complete as possible. It must also be reliable in the sense of being replicable by the same and different examiners, and it should be based on objective criteria.

Neurological examinations of children have been carried out by many examiners and this has resulted in variations in the design of the technique according to personal preferences and tastes. It would be impossible to construct a method which would incorporate all the many tests that have been described. A compromise is inevitable. The reasons for our selection of tests are outlined below.

The least problematic aspect of the neurological examination is the assessment of a large variety of motor functions which, observed in standardized conditions, can be objectively described and quantified. This category comprises posture, spontaneous movements, resistance against passive movements, muscle power, reflexes and locomotion.

Sensory functions which relate to movement can also be easily assessed. These include oculo-motor and pupillary responses, nystagmus, gross pain (withdrawal responses) and proprioceptors (muscle spindles).

However, all those sensory qualities in which perception can only be assessed by verbal report or by imitation are subject to erroneous interpretation because of their dependence on the language development and mental capacity of the patient. Thus, it is extremely difficult to obtain reliable data about light touch or differences in pain perception in children, particularly children with behavioural problems and/or mental deficiency. The examiner will obtain nothing more than vague and subjective impressions. Similar pitfalls hamper the assessment of two-point discrimination and stereognosis, in which the intelligence and motivation of the child play an important rôle.

We found that many of the classical tests of adult neurology were not sensitive enough to detect disturbances in children with relatively minor dysfunction. In children with more severe neurological disorder, *e.g.* hemiplegia, it may be possible to use the classical tests of sensory function to identify a gross sensory loss such as the loss of light touch all over the hemiplegic limb. Even in these circumstances, however, an assessment will only be reliable if the child is old enough and sufficiently intelligent and well-motivated to reply to the examiner's questions. In children with behavioural difficulties, too, we found it very difficult to account for the findings with, for example, two-point discrimination, even in nine- to ten-year-old children. The responses obtained were inconsistent and unreliable from one examination to the next. We feel, therefore, that such tests are not worth carrying out in these children as a routine. In individual cases, it may be useful to carry out a separate, extensive examination of sensory functions.

Clearly, the examiner must be aware that an investigation of one function necessarily involves the use of others. This is important when a child does not pass a test. If he wishes to give an unequivocal interpretation of the finding, the examiner must try to ascertain the cause of the child's failure. For example, in a test of visual acuity such as the Snellen Letter Charts, the Sheridan-Gardner tests or even picture charts, the child's success indicates that visual acuity has been tested. However, in the case of failure the examiner must remember that the test investigates not only visual acuity but also the child's ability to recognise objects and to verbalize. Failure does not necessarily imply impaired visual acuity, particularly in the case of children with behavioural difficulties who may show short attention span and poor concentration. These factors may considerably affect the child's ultimate score, and it would therefore be preferable to refer such children to an ophthalmologist, who can often obtain better and more objective data about visual acuity by skiascopy.

A distinction should be made between deviant findings which are interpretable in terms of neural mechanisms and those which are multiply determined, because learning, social conditions and innumerable other environmental factors influence the performance. The result of a tap on the patellar tendon can be easily related to particular neural mechanisms, but visual acuity depends on many factors.

The same can be said of many tests used in the assessment of motor co-ordination. If a child is asked to pick up matches and put them in a match-box, the examiner may get an impression of his ability to manipulate small objects. The quantification of the performance per time unit in terms of the number of matches placed accurately in the box (most of the items in the Oseretsky battery are of this type) does not make it an unequivocal neurological test because of the many ways in which the results can be interpreted. In addition to motor co-ordination, many other factors are involved, such as visuomotor abilities, general intelligence, motivation and attention span.

The Körper Co-ordination Test for Children (Kiphard and Schilling 1970) and the Imitation of Gestures Test (Bergès and Lézine 1965) measure achievement but do not explain the cause of a poor performance. Obviously, such tests are useful if they differentiate between normal and deviant children, but the type and cause of the deviation must subsequently be analysed by means of the neurological examination.

In designing a specific technique for the neurological examination, it is clearly necessary to obviate complex behavioural data masquerading as neurological items. For instance, if an unspecific hyperkinesis is evaluated as an abnormal neurological *symptom*, then despite our lack of knowledge about its organic basis, this type of behavioural difficulty will automatically be interpreted as a neurological *sign*. Fluctuating attention or a short attention span, whether observed or reported in the history, cannot be taken as evidence of brain dysfunction *per se*. If a child has neurological signs which clearly indicate brain dysfunction, one may surmise that there is an organic basis for the behavioural problems. However, definite proof will still be missing.

In our selection of tests, we have tried to look at as many aspects of

9

neurological function as possible, and to use more than one test to assess each aspect. In some instances it would be possible to extend the number of tests used. For example, many more reflexes than are described here could easily be incorporated. However, we feel that an increase in the number of reflexes tested in a routine examination does not correspondingly increase the amount of information obtained, and we have excluded them for practical reasons.

The child's speech and language deserve special comment. This aspect of behaviour is clearly of particular interest to the developmental neurologist and to all doctors who deal with children. Some types of speech disorders can be specifically related to brain damage, as is well known from adult neurology. Delayed and abnormal speech development in children may arouse a strong suspicion of neurological damage, although it is difficult to be certain that neurological damage is the cause of the abnormality. An accurate assessment of speech and language requires a skilled technique. It is a task for someone with special experience in assessing this particular function and should not be included within the general neurological examination. For clinical purposes, it is often possible to get a general impression of the child's speech during the course of the examination and to refer the child for a separate, detailed examination of this function, if this is judged desirable. However, when examining minor neurological dysfunctions in a specific population for research purposes, it is mandatory to include formal tests by specialists.

One final point which must be considered is the distinction that is often made between 'soft' (or 'equivocal') and 'hard' (or 'unequivocal') signs. As there are no objective criteria for such a distinction, it is open to serious doubt. It is maintained that signs may be considered soft or hard on the basis of elicitation or interpretation. Rutter *et al.* (1970) and Rutter (1977) say that some signs, such as strabismus, may be caused by either neurological dysfunction or non-neurological dysfunction, whilst other soft signs are really mild neurological signs which can be interpreted in an analogous way to the well-known signs of cerebral palsy such as reflex differences. Still other signs, such as slight inco-ordination or clumsy motility, are even too mild for such an interpretation.

In our opinion, the distinction between soft and hard signs is artificial and depends mainly on the point of view of the examiner. As far as we are concerned, the only criterion for the acknowledgement of a neurological sign is its ability to be elicited and replicated by various experienced examiners using standardized techniques. The fact that some signs may fluctuate in intensity over time and may be difficult to establish does not refute this statement; rather, it emphasizes the need for repeated examinations of those children suspected of brain dysfunction.

The interpretation of any sign can be manifold (as with the Babinski response), especially when pathogenesis is looked for. Strabismus, however, is a fairly obvious sign, even though its neurological significance is not yet clear. In our opinion, a finding may be regarded as a neurological sign when it is found in a patient rather than in a healthy individual, even though we often do not know the nature of the relationship (if any) between the sign and the disorder. One of the aims of this book is to make an analysis of such relationships feasible.

Another distinction which is often made is between 'minor' and 'major' signs, based on the presence or absence of obvious handicaps in daily life. A spasticity which handicaps a child's gait is called a major sign, whilst choreiform dyskinesia, which at first glance does not hamper the child as much, is called a minor sign, even though this latter may be very handicapping for fine manipulations and good handwriting. The Babinski reflex is considered a minor sign when it is part of a mild, non-invalidating syndrome, but is considered to be a major sign in the case of a serious pyramidal tract lesion.

Although the labels 'major' and 'minor' seem harmless in comparison with the terms 'soft' and 'hard', they are nevertheless too interpretative and should be avoided as much as possible.

ESSENTIAL CONSIDERATIONS

Developmental Approach

The nervous system of an infant or child is in a phase of rapid development and therefore the examiner's approach must be age-specific. It is essential for him to be familiar with the maturational processes of motor patterns and sensory mechanisms. Our technique is adapted to the maturation of the nervous system from its early stages of relatively low organisation to the increasing organisation of later stages. This type of examination is based on concepts and techniques fundamentally different from those applied in paediatric neurology which have been extrapolated from adult neurology.

In addition, great caution should be exercised if neurophysiological data derived from animal experiments are applied as analogous. For example, an analysis of patterns of spasticity in the cat should not be used as an explanation of the patterns seen in a child. There is evidence of gross differences of nervous functioning between species, and erroneous conclusions may easily be drawn if infantile brain mechanisms are interpreted on the basis of animal studies (Prechtl and Lenard 1968, Geschwind 1974, Touwen 1976).

Behavioural State

The behavioural state of the child is an important variable which greatly influences the results of the examination. With regard to the young infant, an accurate evaluation of the behavioural state during the examination is essential for an interpretation of the findings (Prechtl 1977). For example, an increased resistance to passive movements found in a vigorously moving, crying infant may mean something quite different from the same finding in a quiet or even sleeping infant. Similarly, the behavioural state of pre-school and school-age children must also be taken into account. Clearly, the examination is only possible if the child is awake and therefore his behavioural state need only be recorded in terms of the degree of disturbance. Generally speaking, the type of disturbance found in children aged three to five years is characteristically different from that found in children aged six years and over. Whilst the younger child may react initially with fright and then fuss or cry, the older child may manifest his misgivings in tenseness and rigidity. Obviously, the examiner must try to overcome these reactions before commencing the examination. Should he fail to pacify a crying child, the examination must be

11

discontinued. An older child can be helped to relax by having a play session before the examination.

The scale for behavioural states is given in Table II. The child's state must be recorded on the proforma (p. 125) at the beginning of each section of the examination. Changes of state during the examination can be recorded in a special column on the right side of the proforma. The optimal states for each test are mentioned in the text.

In contrast to the examination of the young infant, there is a second aspect of the behavioural state which plays an important rôle in the assessment of children: the co-operation of the child may determine the validity of the findings. Obviously, this will relate to his behavioural state as described above. Co-operation is expressed in terms of social responsiveness, *i.e.* the way in which the child responds to the examiner's handling and instructions. In this context the scoring is mainly concerned with the validity of the neurological findings and not with a psychiatric appraisal of the child's behaviour. It is sufficient to cover the range of manifestations from positive to negative, using unequivocal descriptions of behaviour that might influence test results, without making any inferences about the underlying mechanisms of that behaviour. The scale for social responsiveness is given in Table III and must be recorded at the end of each section of the examination. Changes in social responsiveness during the course of a section can be noted in a special column on the right side of the proforma opposite the relevant items.

It is, of course, important to keep the child as co-operative as possible during the examination. Tests which are least likely to disturb him are carried out first, and all procedures which might excite or frighten him are postponed to the end. This technique results in a sequence of tests which is in no way logical (as is usual in adult neurology) in terms of brain topography or of functional systems, but which does help to avoid many difficulties.

As the child's behavioural state may be influenced by fatigue, the time at which the examination is carried out must be recorded. It is also necessary to obtain adequate information about factors such as drugs taken by the child and the time of his last meal, as these may influence not only his behavioural state but also the results of the tests.

Tiredness can also influence a child's performance, particularly on tests of

TABLE II

Behavioural state

0* = awake, not crying, relaxed
1 = awake, not crying, tense and rigid
2 = awake, fussing
3 = awake, crying**
4 = yelling**
5 = other (describe)***

* *Scale starts with '0' for reasons of coding on punch cards.*
** *If crying or yelling persists for any length of time, the examination procedure must be discontinued.*
*** *Fatigue, for example, can be coded here.*

12

TABLE III
Social responsiveness

0* = interested, agrees with proposals, no stimulation needed, facial expression alert.
1 = disinterested, but agrees with proposals, no particular encouragement needed, but not facially alert.
2 = reluctant, needs encouragement, appears anxious, tense facial expression.
3 = reluctant, needs encouragement, appears sullen, withdrawn.
4 = shrinks back on approach, refuses to fulfill demands, appears frightened.
5 = refuses to fulfill demands, appears impassive.
6 = resists by pushing examiner away, tries to get away, struggles.
7 = other (describe).

*Scale starts with '0' for reasons of coding on punch cards.

manipulative ability and dyskinesia, and our experience has shown that it may be necessary to test a child at two different times of the day (early morning and late afternoon perhaps) in order to compare the findings. Moreover, it must be remembered that the period of the year (just before or just after holidays) or a particular circumstance (a forthcoming birthday for instance) can also influence performance (Stemmer 1964).

Environmental Conditions and Technique of Handling the Patient

The behavioural state of the child is strongly influenced by environmental conditions and these need to be standardized. Certain aspects of special importance are discussed here, as some doctors tend to consider them minor points and disregard them, which may account for difficulties in obtaining reliable results.

Undressing

In general, children dislike being undressed during the examination. Young children get particularly tense and this may impede a reliable assessment. This difficulty will diminish in the case of older children over the age of seven, although boys are often extremely bashful and tense during the examination of the cremasteric reflex.

To alleviate these problems, undressing should be adapted to the needs of the examination. The child does not need to remain undressed the whole time, and in our experience it is preferable that he should stay undressed for as short a time as possible.* However, he should take off his shoes and socks at the beginning of the examination and remain barefoot throughout, otherwise accurate observation of posture and motility of the feet and legs is not possible. Muscle power and resistance to passive movements can be tested before the child removes any more clothing; for the testing of tendon reflexes, he must remove outer clothing so that his arms and legs are bare; and the examination of the trunk requires further undressing. Obviously, undressing in stages will take up more time, but this is compensated for by the child's improved social responsiveness and loss of tension.

*The children appearing in the illustrations are undressed in many instances in order to demonstrate the procedures and responses more clearly.

13

It is often advisable for the examiner, rather than the mother or nurse, to help the child get dressed again, as many children find this reassuring. Once the child is dressed and convinced of the friendly nature of the examination, the assessment of the head (funduscopy, testing of the corneal and gag reflexes and inspection of the pharyngeal arches), which often frightens young children, can be carried out with relative ease. We ourselves have never found any difficulty in carrying out a funduscopic examination, for example, since by the end of the session the child is usually relaxed and co-operative.

The Examination Couch

Many children, particularly those under six years of age, are frightened by examination couches which are usually too high, narrow and cold. However, most items of the neurological examination can be tested while the child is sitting or standing. If a couch is absolutely essential, it should be reasonably low and broad, and covered with a soft mattress. A mat on the floor often provides the best means of carrying out parts of the examination when the child has to lie down (*e.g.* the knee-heel test, testing of the hip joints, inspection of the spine and the posture of the legs in prone and supine positions). The abdominal skin, Galant and cremasteric reflexes are elicitable, when present, in the standing child. It is also easier to examine muscle power, resistance against passive movements (in most joints) and reflexes (all of which require a relaxed subject) when the child is sitting rather than lying down. For this purpose, an ordinary wooden chair without arms can generally be used. The child's feet must not touch the floor, so older children may have to sit on the edge of the table; a music-stool of adjustable height may also be used, provided its surface is not round and convex, since this would influence the child's sitting posture. Certain specific tests, such as tests for dyskinesia and diadochokinesis, are best done when the child is standing.

The Examination Room

Clearly, the room where the examination takes place should be quiet and restful, so that the child can feel at ease. A doctor's examination room often contains a certain amount of frightening paraphernalia, and this should be removed, as should the examiner's white coat. In addition, the room (and the examiner's hands) should be pleasantly warm.

The Presence of the Mother

The advisability of allowing a parent or other familiar adult to be present during the examination has been much disputed, and often depends more on the examiner than on the child. General rules cannot be given but, for the examination of groups with an aim to statistical analysis, it is advisable to keep the environmental situation the same in all cases. We would therefore suggest that mothers of children up to the age of six should be asked to be present, while older children should be seen alone.

Relationship with the Child

The initial moments of the interview often determine the course of the examination, and we have found that it is important not to approach the young child directly at the beginning. An introductory talk to the mother while the child is listening and playing with a toy placed near him by the examiner will often impress the child more than a direct explanation. After a few minutes the examiner may make a direct remark to the child, who by this time has had time to familiarize himself with his surroundings. An adequate period of adaptation should be allowed and it might be worthwhile noting its duration. During this period, the examiner can observe posture and motility, which may give clues to be followed up at a later phase of the examination.

It is important that the examination procedure should be playful wherever possible (in the examination of muscle power, for instance) so as to reassure the child. The order of the examination was designed with this in mind.

Another point that the examiner should consider is that he is likely to tower above the sitting and even the standing child. He should therefore avoid standing up or leaning over the child, but should sit or squat beside or opposite him. When he has to move around, he should do so as inconspicuously as possible.

THE COURSE OF THE EXAMINATION

The examination consists of (1) an observation of the child's motor behaviour, and (2) testing of specific nervous functions.

In general, the examiner should keep to the course of the examination as set out in this book. The procedure is divided into several sections. All the items which can be assessed while the child is sitting down are carried out first, followed by an examination while the child is standing. Locomotion is then tested. An assessment in the lying position is left almost to the end of the procedure, and is followed by the last section, namely, the examination of the head.

At the beginning and end of each section, the child's behavioural state and degree of social responsiveness are always recorded. If the child's state changes during a section, or if a specific test (*e.g.* for dyskinesia) requires an additional assessment, then a subsequent recording is necessary. The examiner should allow himself some degree of flexibility within each section and remember that his main aim is to ensure that the child is not disturbed by the examination and remains as responsive as possible.

This method is specifically designed for the detection of minor neurological dysfunction, and in the discussion of the findings most emphasis is placed on their meaning in relation to minor dysfunction. However, mention must be made of their significance in relation to more serious conditions, as minor signs may be the first manifestations of a progressive illness. Single abnormal signs are rarely of much significance in isolation; a comprehensive examination is necessary to evaluate the child's neurological status. One should always approach the interpretation of single tests with care, but for practical reasons the possible significance of each test is mentioned after a description of the procedure and recording.

Each test item of the proforma in each section is discussed separately, and in each case relevant age variables are mentioned, the technique of eliciting a response is described (*i.e.* the position of the child and the examiner, the method of procedure and the response itself), the way of recording the response is indicated, and some remarks are made about the significance of the response and its relationship to the child's age. These remarks do not pretend to give either a complete outline of the significance or a differential diagnosis of all responses. As stated previously, this book is primarily a methodological and not a clinical textbook.

The responses are measured numerically: the absence of a response is always scored as 0, a weak response as 1, a clear response as 2, a strong response as 3, *etc.* This must be taken into account in the final interpretation. In the case of responses which are normally *present*, the optimal score will usually be 2; a weak response which may be non-optimal scores 1; a strong response which may also be non-optimal scores 3 or 4. This applies to tendon reflexes and resistance against passive movements, for example. However, in the case of the plantar grasp response, which should be *absent*, the optimal score will be 0, while scores of 1 or 2 reflect non-optimal responses, *i.e.* the presence of the response.

What is meant by 'non-optimal' signs? As Prechtl (1965, 1968, 1977) has pointed out, it is easier to define what is called an 'optimal' response than to define precisely the difference between 'normal' and 'abnormal' or 'pathological'. The optimal response is the best response obtainable; a non-optimal response is any response which does not meet this criterion. Obviously, optimality of a response is often age-dependent and it is important to stress that non-optimality is not always synonymous with abnormality; an abnormal response is always non-optimal, whilst not every non-optimal response is abnormal. Optimality and normality, on the other hand, often overlap. In the case of reflex intensities, for instance, medium intensity ($++$) is both optimal and normal; negative, low or high intensities ($-$, $+$, $+++$) are non-optimal, but whether they should be considered as borderline-normal or abnormal depends on the combination with other signs. Counting the number of optimal findings is a means of quantifying the integrity of the nervous system. This is particularly valuable in those cases where no traditional diagnosis can be made since no definitely abnormal signs are present in recognisable patterns. The total sum of the optimal findings in the neurological examination is called the optimality score. It can be divided into subscores according to subsystems, as will be described in the paragraph on the neurological profile in Chapter 12.

After the description of the full examination, the interrelation of signs and their cohesion into syndromes is discussed, followed by a critical annotation of their possible relationship to behaviour. It must be stressed again that a single neurological sign very rarely has any clinical significance. Only the number and possible interrelationship of signs can give a guide to the interpretation of results. On completion of the examination, the examiner collates the abnormal signs recorded descriptively during the examination, and attempts to see how they relate and whether they form a recognised syndrome. Quite often he will find a number of unrelated signs and no clear-cut syndrome, so that it may perhaps be possible to speak of a syndrome consisting of the absence of a syndrome.

CHAPTER 4

Assessment of the Child Sitting

General Remarks
     As indicated previously, the behavioural state of the child (Table II, p. 12) should be recorded at the beginning of the examination and at the beginning of each set of tests. Social responsiveness (Table III) should be recorded at the end of each set of tests. Any change in either state or responsiveness during the course of a section should be noted in the appropriate column. It is also worthwhile recording both aspects before and after the child takes off his shoes and socks.

Behavioural State and Social Responsiveness
     In the following series of tests, the child's optimal score for 'behavioural state' is 0 and for 'social responsiveness' it is 0 or 1.

Position
     The child is asked to sit up straight on a chair, without supporting himself with his arms or elbows. The chair should preferably be a simple upright one with no arms. The child's feet should not touch the floor, so older children may have to sit on a table. If the child's posture seems abnormal, it is advisable to ask him to get up and walk around before sitting down again.
     When the child is sitting down, it is very important to see that the head is kept in the midline and that the posture of the body and limbs is symmetrical. A slight tendency towards an asymmetric tonic neck response pattern, for instance, may be present, and this can influence findings. If a child cannot centre his head or keep it centred, this must be recorded. In the case of torticollis, passive centring of the head means a change of tension in the neck muscles on both sides, and this can influence the findings on other tests, as can other postural deviations of the body.

Spontaneous Motility

Age
     This test is suitable for all children between three and 12 years of age.

Procedure
     An observation of spontaneous motility can be carried out initially during the introductory talk to the mother when the child is sitting and playing with a toy. Quantity and quality of movement must be taken into account, and a distinction made between gross and small movements in each instance.
     In *gross movements,* body and limbs all participate. The child may arch his back, move around in the chair, swing his legs, etc. Eventually, gross movements will

17

result in spatial displacements, the child jumping off the chair, walking round the room, climbing over the furniture or opening the door.

In *small movements,* only parts of the body or limbs are involved. The child may be restless and fidget with hands or fingers, make faces, wiggle his toes or fidget with buttons, clothes or other objects, but his position changes relatively little, if at all.

The quantity and quality of the movements are estimated as indicated below, and special attention must be paid to the occurrence of involuntary movements such as tremor, choreiform movements or slight dystonic movements (see page 53).

Recording

(a) *Quantity*

Gross movements:

0 = no movements. The child sits perfectly still for at least three minutes.

1 = a few movements only. The child stays on the chair, but turns around a bit, swings his legs, etc.

2 = a moderate amount of movements. The child stays on the chair, but turns around repeatedly, arches his back and swings his legs.

3 = an excessive amount of movements. The child is continuously on the move, jumps on and off the chair and wanders round the room.

Small movements:

0 = no movements. The child sits perfectly still for at least three minutes.

1 = a few movements only, mainly of hands and face.

2 = a moderate amount of movements. The child moves his hands and feet, but not continuously.

3 = an excessive amount of movements. The child fidgets continuously, cannot keep his hands or feet still, plucks at his clothing, etc.

(b) *Quality*

Speed:

0 = the child sits perfectly still.

1 = the movements are performed slowly.

2 = the movements are performed at a moderate tempo.

3 = all movements are performed very rapidly.

Smoothness:

0 = the child sits perfectly still.

1 = all movements are very smooth and supple.

2 = movements are mostly smooth and supple, often depending on their speed.

	3 = movements are performed clumsily and may be abrupt and jerky, often giving the impression of being broken down into constituent parts.
	4 = all movements are performed very awkwardly or are very abrupt and jerky.
Adequacy:	0 = the child sits perfectly still.
	1 = movements are easily goal-directed.
	2 = some movements are goal-directed, others are inadequate and do not serve a clear purpose.
	3 = the child moves around aimlessly; his movements are mainly inadequate.

(c) *Involuntary movements*

Type and localisation are described if present (see page 53).

Significance

A score of 3 for quantity of gross movements denotes overactivity; a score of 3 for quantity of small movements denotes a restless or fidgety child. However, these descriptions do not indicate a diagnosis of 'hyperkinesis', which is the descriptive term for a behavioural category. It is necessary to record the quantity of spontaneous motility, but it is the quality of movement which is truly significant for an understanding of the child's neurological functioning.

Speed, smoothness and adequacy may not be equally affected; high scores for speed are not always paralleled by high scores for smoothness and adequacy. In some overactive children, all aspects may be scored highly, denoting a rapidly moving child whose movements are jerky and abrupt and often inadequate. Children with awkward and clumsy motility will often show low scores for quantity and speed of movements. Younger children (aged below six) will normally show more movements than older children.

It should be borne in mind that the quality of movement is age-dependent, especially in three- and four-year-old children. Goal-directed movements can often only be performed adequately if the child fixates his shoulder girdle by pressing his elbow against his side (Figs. 32 and 33, p. 62). This behaviour is unusual in older children. Allowance should also be made for the occurrence of associated movements (*e.g.* mirror movements) in three-year-olds, which in older children usually occur only diring the performance of unusual or very difficult movements.

Obviously, if involuntary movements such as choreiform movements or tremor are present, smoothness will be affected, but quantity, speed and adequacy of isolated movements may well be within the normal range.

Once more, it must be stressed that single observations are not a sufficient basis for conclusions which can only be reached after a complete examination. Spontaneous motility is observed again when the child is standing at a later stage in the procedure.

Posture

Age

This test is suitable for children between three and 12 years of age.

Procedure

The examiner inspects the posture of the head, body and legs. He should pay special attention to any tilting or rotation of the head and rotation or bending (either forward or backward) of the spine. A slight scoliosis may pass unobserved, as the child is at this point barefoot but otherwise fully dressed.

Recording

Any persistent deviations from a symmetrical upright posture are described by noting the appropriate score in the relevant place on the proforma. Posture of the head, trunk, legs and feet is scored in the following way:

Head:	rotated		
	bent laterally		
	ante- and retroflexion		
Trunk:	rotated		
	bent laterally		
	kyphosis (describe level)		
	lordosis		
	symmetrically collapsed		
Legs:	endorotation	flexion	abduction
	exorotation	extension	adduction
Feet:	endorotation	dorsiflexion	abduction
	exorotation	plantar flexion	adduction

The scores range from 0 to 2. 0 indicates that the description is not valid; 2 indicates that the description is manifestly valid. Each side of the body is scored separately on the corresponding side of the proforma, unless otherwise indicated. If, for instance, a child sits with one knee slightly more flexed than the other, and this is a consistent finding, the score for the more flexed side would be 1 (often in that instance there will be a slightly increased adduction of the same leg). This does not necessarily indicate an abnormality, but merely records a difference between the two sides.

Significance

In all cases, the optimal score is 0, indicating a neutral posture. Sometimes a child may have slightly bent shoulders which he can hold straight on request but which droop again after a moment; as a rule this is not a pathological finding. A final conclusion can only be reached when the examination of posture while standing and during movement has been completed and after the sensorimotor apparatus has been adequately tested. When a child is sitting, it is quite normal for some degree of lumbar lordosis or thoraco-kyphosis to be present. Lumbar lordosis may be particularly prominent in slender girls.

Children who are slightly hypotonic may sit on the lower end of the back instead of on the buttocks. This is accentuated when the child is asked to extend his knees and straighten his trunk while supporting himself with his arms. If hypertonia of the hamstring muscles is present, the child adducts his legs during this procedure, which is suggestive of a slight diplegia.

A consistently maintained asymmetrical posture should always arouse a suspicion of pathology, which will be confirmed or dispelled during the rest of the examination. Deviations due to obvious bone or muscle deformities need not be mentioned here. A slightly abnormal posture may result from muscular weakness on one or both sides of the body. Lateral incurvations of the trunk may indicate a scoliosis, and this must be checked when the child is standing and lying down.

Lateral turning of the head may be due to visual difficulties, *e.g.* suppression of diplopia (originating from paresis of the musculus rectus lateralis of one eye) or compensation for a homonymous hemianopia.

An asymmetrical posture of the freely hanging legs, often most clearly indicated by the position of the feet, may originate from or be one of the first manifestations of a hemisyndrome (see page 109). On the other hand, static causes (originating in the hip joint, the ankle or the foot) must also be borne in mind.

Reaction to Push against the Shoulder while Sitting

Age
This test is suitable for all ages, if performed in a playful manner.

Procedure
While the child is sitting upright, with his hands on his knees and his head centred, the examiner gives a gentle sideward push against the child's shoulder. The ability of the child to remain in a sitting position is recorded. The intensity of the push is graded according to the child's age.

Response
The child will try to keep his balance by shifting his body to the ipsilateral side. He may lift one or both hands from his knees, and may even use one hand for lateral support. The examiner should take care to prevent the child from toppling over.

Recording
    0 = the child falls sideways and must be caught.
    1 = the child lifts his arms and uses his opposite hand for lateral support.
    2 = the child lifts his hands from his knees.
    3 = the child keeps his balance without moving arms or hands.

Significance
In children up to six years of age, scores 2 and 3 can be considered optimal; in older children score 3 is optimal. An inability to perform this test may be caused by an abnormality of muscle tone (hypo- or hypertonia), by postural abnormalities, or by

disturbances of trunk co-ordination of either cerebellar or proprioceptive origin. In these last two types of dysfunction, swaying movements (oscillation or overshooting) are often conspicuous.

Following an Object with Rotation of the Trunk while Sitting

Age
This test is suitable for children of all ages.

Position
As in the foregoing test.

Procedure
The examiner holds an interesting object, such as a small toy, to the side of and slightly behind the child's head. He asks the child to look at the object and then to grasp it. The presence or absence of trunk rotation during the child's movements is recorded.

Response
The child will turn his head and rotate his shoulders to the side where the object is presented, while his hips remain more or less centered. Some compensatory balancing movements of the legs (spreading the knees, deviation of the legs to the contralateral side) may be observed especially in children below seven years old.

Recording
> 0 = the child cannot turn to the object without supporting himself on his hand.
> 1 = the child rotates his whole trunk without differentiation between shoulders and hips. Compensatory movements of the legs present.
> 2 = some rotation visible from the shoulders to the hips, often associated with compensatory movements of the legs.
> 3 = good rotation of the trunk while maintaining a stable sitting position.

Significance
Trunk rotation should be present at three years, but sitting balance without arm/hand support during rotation may still be difficult at that age. However, rotation of the head must be possible over about 180°.

Deficient balance may be due to deviations of muscle tone or co-ordination of the trunk, of cerebellar (or, rarely, proprioceptive) origin. In the latter case swaying movements (oscillations or overshooting movements) are usually present. Deficient rotation of the shoulders to the pelvis may be due to an excess of stretch reflex activity in the back muscles. It must be borne in mind that the muscle tone can be found to be normal or hypotonic during the examination of the motor system. In this case, deficient rotation may be the only sign of a deviation in the sensorimotor system of central origin. It may be an early sign of a progressive disorder or merely a sign of non-progressive minor neurological dysfunction. In these cases, a general 'clumsiness' is conspicuous.

Skeletal abnormality must be excluded.

ASSESSMENT OF THE MOTOR SYSTEM

Age

These tests are suitable for all children between the ages of three and 10 years of age.

General Remarks

The assessment is divided into three aspects: active power, resistance against passive movements and range of movements. The neck, shoulders, elbows, wrists, knees and ankles are tested separately for all three categories. Examination of the hip-joint is postponed until the end of the examination when the child is lying on the examination table.

French authors such as André-Thomas *et al.* (1960) and Tardieu (1968) have made valuable contributions to the study of tone, and many tests have been described for use in such an assessment. We feel that many of these tests are difficult to standardize, and that as much information can be gained from the use of much simpler tests.

Behavioural State and Social Responsiveness

A score of 0 is optimal for both categories, though for social responsiveness a score of 1 is also acceptable.

Muscle Power

Procedure

The child is asked to grasp the examiner's fingers as tightly as possible, using both hands at the same time. The examiner must resist voluntary flexion and extension of the elbow. Abduction and adduction of the arm against resistance provides an estimation of the power of the arm and shoulder muscles.

Pronation and supination should be carefully tested as, in its early stages, a paresis may manifest itself in the muscles used for these movements (*e.g.* in muscular dystrophy). The examiner must take hold of the child's hand as if to shake hands and ask him to pronate and supinate against resistance. (Pronation is usually stronger than supination.)

The strength of the hip and thigh muscles is examined at the end of the procedure when the child is lying on the examination table (for flexion, extension, abduction and adduction). Flexion and extension of the knee joint and the strength of the ankle and foot movements can be tested while the child is sitting.

After testing for power of movement against resistance, the child is asked to keep the various joints still while the examiner tries to move them.

Recording

The muscle power tested in these two ways is recorded as a compound score for each joint (see proforma p. 126). We feel that the well-known Medical Research Council scale is not really useful in the case of children with minor dysfunction of the nervous system, since such children are unlikely to exhibit muscular weakness so severe that they are unable to make movements against gravity. Several ratings of the MRC scale have therefore been omitted, but approximate equivalents to our own scale are given in brackets.

0 = no active movements (MRC 0, 1, 2 and partially 3).

1 = active movements present, but unable to overcome more than slight resistance (MRC partially 3 and 4).

2 = active movements present, and able to counteract moderately strong resistance (MRC 5).

3 = active movements present, and able to overcome very strong resistance (MRC partially 5).

Resistance against Passive Movements (Figs. 1-6).

Procedure

The child is asked to relax as much as possible, and resistance is tested and assessed by passively moving the various joints.

The examiner first takes the child's head in his hands and gently bends it forward, backward and to each side. The shoulder joint is tested by holding the shoulder girdle firm with one hand and moving the child's upper arm through the range of movements of the shoulder joint with the other. To test the elbow, the upper arm is held firm while the lower arm is flexed and extended; to test the wrist joint, the lower arm is held firm in a semiflexed position (to avoid pronation and supination which is tested separately) and the hand is moved.

While the child is sitting, the position of the hip joint can be standardized by holding the upper leg firm, so that the resistance of the knee can be tested. To test the ankle joint, the lower leg is held firm with the knee in a semiflexed position.

The passive movements must be carried out slowly and carefully, and should be repeated several times.

Recording

Resistance against passive movements is recorded as a compound score for each joint (see proforma, page 126).

0 = complete lack of resistance.

1 = weak resistance.

2 = moderately strong resistance.

3 = strong resistance.

Range of Passive Movements

Procedure

In testing resistance to passive movements, the joints are moved through their

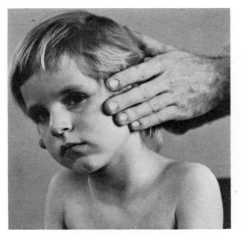

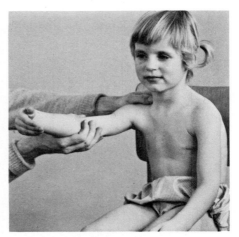

Fig. 1. Examination of resistance to passive movements in the neck. The head is gently moved to the side.

Fig. 2. Examination of resistance to passive movements in the right shoulder.

full range, and hyperextensibility or limitation of movements is recorded. The range of movements shows wide individual variation. The average range of movements for the various joints is as follows:

Head	Anteflexion:	the chin can touch the chest.
	Retroflexion:	an imaginary plane from mentum to occiput approaches the horizontal.
	Rotation:	180° from side to side.
Shoulder	Abduction:	to ± 110° with shoulder girdle held firm.
	Anteflexion:	to ± 100° with shoulder girdle held firm.
	Retroflexion:	to ± 60° with shoulder girdle held firm.
	Other movements are not considered.	
Elbow	Extension:	to 180°.
	Flexion:	to ± 20°, depending on the thickness of the arm.
Wrist	Extension:	to 70° with lower arm.
	Flexion:	to 90° with lower arm.
Knees	Extension:	to 180°.
	Flexion:	depending on the bulk of the leg.
Ankles	The range of movement from dorsiflexion to plantar flexion is 100°/110°.	

Recording

Only the degree of deviation from the average range of movements described above is recorded, and this is quantified as far as is possible by using a goniometer for instance (Holt 1965).

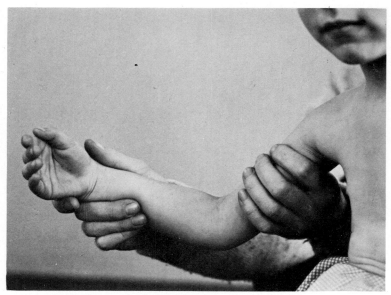

Fig. 3. Examination of resistance to passive movements in the right elbow.

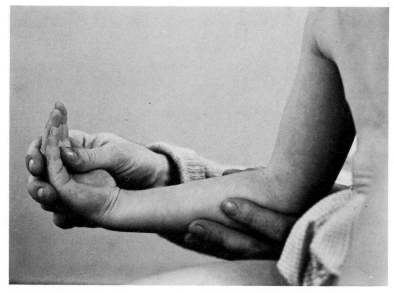

Fig. 4. Examination of resistance to passive movements in the right wrist and hand.

26

Significance

Decreased active power may result from neuromuscular disease, paresis or general weakness or it could be a symptom of an infectious disease, a metabolic disturbance or malnutrition. A slight decrease in muscle strength may be the first manifestation of a progressive disorder, and cases of unilateral decrease should be noted with particular care. The examiner must try to discover whether the muscle weakness has a central or peripheral origin. It should be remembered that a central paresis in young children need not be accompanied by an increased resistance to passive movements. Usually, the results of the assessment of the tendon reflexes and the exteroceptive responses (*e.g.* Mayer and Léri reflexes, plantar response) will help to differentiate between a central, peripheral and myogenic weakness.

A thorough discussion of the causes of increased and decreased resistance against passive movements is beyond the scope of this book, which is principally concerned with minor, often inconspicuous, deviations from optimal functioning. Nevertheless, the examiner must bear in mind that in extreme cases, a slight alteration in resistance to passive movements may be one of the first signs of a progressive disorder of the neuromuscular system (*e.g.* leucodystrophies, cerebro-retinal degenerations, dyskinesias such as Huntington's chorea, cerebral neoplasms or toxic degenerations such as lead poisoning).

Table IV provides a review of the main causes of neuromuscular weakness in childhood. It should be noted that disturbances of the afferent input to the spinal cord (afferent nerves, spinal ganglion, dorsal roots or dorsal columns) may result in a decreased resistance to passive movements before other signs are present. In cases of hypotonia, not all muscles are necessarily involved at the same time. One may be impaired while others function normally, *e.g.* the peroneal muscle of the lower leg (see test for walking on heels, page 77).

A decreased resistance against passive movements is often found in mentally retarded children. Children who turn out to be spastic at the age of two to three years may also show a decreased resistance against passive movements during early infancy. On the other hand, a slight decrease of resistance to passive movements may be found in young pre-school children and may disappear in the course of the years.

TABLE IV

Causes of neuromuscular weakness in childhood

(a) Unspecific:	infectious diseases
	metabolic disorders
	malnutrition
	convalescence from
	   serious illness
		(c) Neuropathies
		
		(d) Disorders of the neuromuscular
		     junction: myasthenia gravis

(b) Disorders of the C.N.S.:
   perinatal C.N.S. damage
   leucodystrophies
   metabolic disorders·
   myelopathies
		(e) Myopathies: muscular dystrophies
		     (dermato) myositis
		     congenital non-progressive
		     myopathies
		     myotonic syndromes
		     periodic paralysis

N.B. Adapted from Munsat and Pearson 1967.

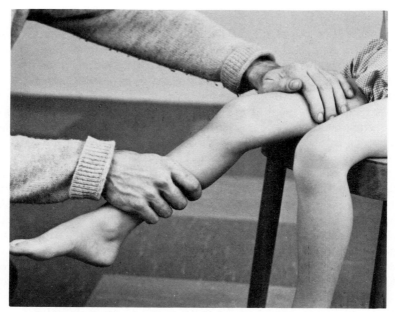

Fig. 5. Examination of resistance to passive movements in the right knee.

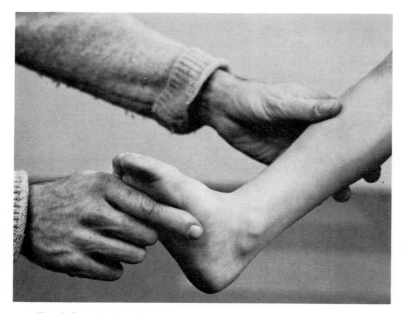

Fig. 6. Examination of resistance to passive movements in the right foot.

28

Generally speaking, a child's resistance to passive movements depends to a certain degree on his soma type and muscle bulk. Girls often show a level of resistance to passive movements which, while normal for them, would be considered low in boys.

It is also beyond the scope of this book to discuss the differentiation between spasticity, 'lead-pipe' rigidity and 'cog-wheel' rigidity, since these phenomena evidently surpass the bounds of minor neurological dysfunction. An increased resistance to passive movements, if not of central nervous system origin, may be due to myogenic (scleroderma, acute myositis) or articular (acute or chronic rheumatoid arthritis) disorders. Conclusions as to origin and diagnosis in an individual patient can only be made when the examination has been completed.

Particularly in five- to eight-year-old children, a slight but consistent discrepancy can sometimes be found in the resistance against passive movements between the left and right limbs. Often there seems to exist a relationship with handedness and footedness, which at this stage of the examination has not been assessed. Usually the preferred arm and leg show greater resistance. It may be that the discrepancy is the result of a differential development of the muscle-bulk on the preferred side. It is also possible, however, that the complete assessment may reveal signs that constitute a definite pattern with which such a discrepancy is congruent, indicating the presence of a hemisyndrome (see page 109).

The range of movements of the joints may vary considerably from child to child, especially with regard to the degree of extension. Slender girls have wider ranges of movements than more heavily-built boys of the same age. Children aged three to four may have a slightly smaller range of movements than children aged four and over, whose muscular system is better developed. A classic case is the three-year-old with a rather protruberant belly and slightly rounded shoulders, who often shows a slightly decreased range of movements of the joints. However, between the ages of four and seven, flexibility of the joints is not related to age; variations commonly occur not only between children but also between the various joints of the individual child. The ethnic background should also be noted, as children of Asian or Eurasian parents often show a greater range of movements than Caucasian children of the same age.

An abnormal increase in the range of movements is generally related to a low resistance against passive movements. Limitation of movements may originate in the ligaments of the joints, the muscles or the motor neurons. Complaints of pain during the examination should be very carefully investigated. Testing the range of movements may be painful, particularly where there are articular or myogenic limitations of movement, and this pain may in turn cause further limitation of movement during the examination. Spontaneous pain caused by acute arthritis or dermomyositis, for example, or even from any other origin, may decrease the range of movements by causing an inability to relax the musculature, thus interfering with the optimal range of movements basically present. Persistent asymmetries should always be carefully considered, since they may be part of a hemisyndrome. This conclusion can only be drawn on completion of the entire examination, when other causes (*e.g.* local or peripheral) can be excluded.

Kicking

Age

This test is suitable for children aged three to six, and for older children who fail the knee-heel test (see page 87).

Procedure

The examiner holds out his hand on a level with the child's knee at such a distance that the child can easily touch it with his foot. The child is asked to touch the examiner's palm with his toes. The test is carried out with the hand in three positions for each foot; first the examiner holds out his hand directly in front of the child and the child is asked to kick three times; then he holds out his hand at a 45° angle to the left and then to the right of the child for three kicks each time.

Response

The child kicks the examiner's hand, scoring a point for each hit. The highest score for each leg is thus 9.

Recording

The number of kicks for each leg is recorded quantitatively in each position, so that the total score can be quickly calculated.

Significance

This is mainly a test of the co-ordination of the legs for children who cannot or will not do the knee-heel test. A discrepancy between right and left may be related to dominance, and an interpretation is only possible in combination with findings from the rest of the examination. Performance is correlated with age; the child can normally perform perfectly with both legs by the age of five years.

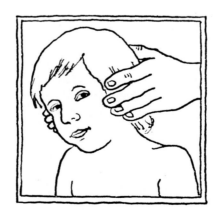

CHAPTER 5

Examination of Reflexes

General Remarks

During the examination of many reflexes (including the plantar reflex, abdominal skin reflex and cremasteric reflex, which are tested at a later stage), the examiner should bear in mind that the response may diminish after two or more trials. If several trials are needed for the same reflex, there should be an interval (sometimes lasting a few minutes) between each trial.

Behavioural State and Social Responsiveness

The optimal behavioural state and responsiveness for the child in the following tests is 0, though one can proceed if the score for responsiveness is 1.

Position

The child may remain sitting on the table or chair. During the elicitation of reflexes, the posture of the arms and legs should be symmetrical and the child's head should be centred in the midline, in order to avoid the differential influences of asymmetric postures (especially of the head and trunk) on the test results.

Age

These tests are suitable for all children between three and 12 years of age.

Ankle Jerk (Fig. 7)

Procedure

We have found that most children are more relaxed when sitting than when lying on an examination table or kneeling on a chair. The muscles of the child's knee and ankle joints should be relaxed for the test. The examiner then grasps the child's foot and keeps it in a neutral position in relation to the child's leg so that he can control the degree of relaxation by slightly moving the foot and leg. Moreover, he can vary the posture in order to find the position of knee and ankle joints which seem best for the elicitation of the ankle jerk. Using a reflex hammer, the examiner taps on the Achilles tendon about 2 to 3cm above the insertion at the calcaneus. If there is no response, he should vary the relative positions of knee and ankle joints, bearing in mind that the gastrocnemius muscle (which is largely responsible for the ankle jerk) covers both knee and ankle joints. If a positive response is obtained, the examiner repeats the tap a number of times, varying the intensity of the tap and varying the distance from the insertion of the tendon. In this way he can evaluate the reflex threshold. Although there is a difference between a low threshold (evaluated by taps of varying intensity) and the extension of the reflexogenic area (evaluated by tapping at varying distances from the original spot), these two are so closely correlated that for practical purposes

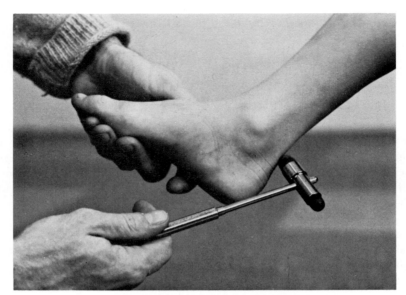

Fig. 7. Elicitation of the Achilles tendon reflex.

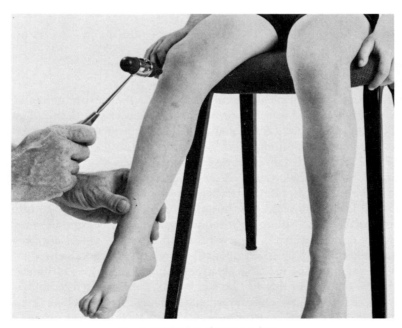

Fig. 8. Elicitation of the knee jerk.

they are considered comparable. The common technique for the elicitation of the ankle jerk, which consists in asking the patient to kneel on the chair or table with his feet dangling, is usually of no use with children, as they do not relax easily in that position.

Response

A brief plantar flexion of the foot at the ankle may be observed. In nervous children it is sometimes accompanied by a slight flexion of the knees and/or toes.

Recording

    0 = absent.
    1 = weak.
    2 = moderate.
    3 = brisk, sometimes followed by a few clonic beats.
    4 = sustained clonus >7-8 beats.

Knee Jerk (Fig. 8)

Procedure

The examiner crouches in front of the child, and takes the child's leg in one hand, making sure that the knee joint is relaxed by gently moving the leg. He keeps the knee in a semiflexed position, and gives a short tap with the reflex hammer on the patellar tendon ± 1cm below the patella. It is important to check the spot, as a tap slightly to the side of the tendon will often result in a poor response. If no response is obtained, the examiner changes the degree of flexion of the knee joint until he finds the position which gives the best result. If a positive response is obtained, the examiner varies the intensity of the tap and the distance from the patella (on or below the insertion of the quadriceps tendon at the tibia) and above the patella on the muscle itself, in order to evaluate the reflex threshold.

Response

A quick extension of the knee, caused by contraction of the quadriceps muscle, may be observed. Younger children may also show a slight adductor contraction, generally in the opposite leg, but occasionally in both the opposite and the stimulated leg. The presence of any adductor contraction should be recorded separately for each side. Three-year-old children may sometimes show some hip flexion.

Recording

    0 = absent.
    1 = weak.
    2 = moderate.
    3 = exaggerated response, sometimes followed by a few clonic beats and/or adduction of the opposite and/or stimulated leg.
    4 = sustained clonus; evident adduction of both legs.
  (If the knee jerk is pendular, this is recorded separately.)

Biceps Reflex (Fig. 9)

Procedure

The child is asked to put his flexed arms on his lap so that the elbows are in a neutral position. The examiner ascertains for himself that the elbow joints are relaxed by gently moving the child's forearms. He places a finger on the tendon of the child's biceps muscle, and gives a short tap on this finger with the reflex hammer. If no response is obtained, the degree of flexion of the elbow must be varied until the position which furnishes the best response is reached. The test should be repeated with taps of varying intensity and at varying distances from the elbow—higher up the upper arm on the biceps tendon and muscle bulk, and by tapping on the lower arm, along the volar side—in order to evaluate the reflex threshold. By keeping the position of the arms symmetrical during the elicitation of the reflex, the results on both sides can be compared directly.

Response

A quick flexion of the elbow, caused by the contraction of the biceps muscle, may be seen and/or felt. Often the brachialis muscle also contracts and the response (flexion of the forearm) is more evident. If the brachialis radialis muscle (situated at the radial side of the forearm and the biceps tendon) is stimulated, a slight pronation of the forearm may occur. Many children show a gentle flexion of the fingers, especially if the forearm is kept supinated, though this response—which means a spreading of the stimulus to other muscles—is not necessarily present. Sometimes, however, a slight flexion of the fingers is the only response to be observed, especially in children with biceps reflexes of low intensity. In this case we interpret the flexion of the fingers as a positive response of low intensity of the biceps reflex, but only if the position of the elbow joint is sufficiently varied to guarantee that no better response can be obtained.

Recording

    0 = absent.
    1 = weak, felt but not seen.
    2 = moderate movements of elbow, often slight flexion of the fingers and/ or slight pronation of the forearm.
    3 = exaggerated response; sometimes a few clonic beats; generally a marked flexion of the fingers whether the forearm is kept supinated or not.

Triceps Reflex (Fig. 10)

Procedure

The examiner takes the child's wrist in one hand so that the elbow is semiflexed, and confirms that the elbow and shoulder muscles are relaxed by gently moving these joints. He taps with the reflex hammer on the tendon of the triceps muscle about 1 to 2cm above the olecranon. The test should be repeated with taps of varying intensity on the tendon and muscle at a greater distance from the olecranon, in order to evaluate the reflex threshold.

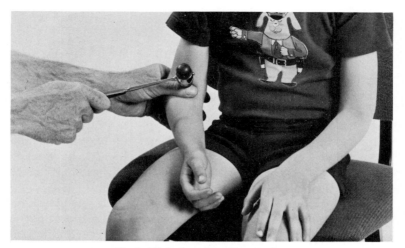

Fig. 9. Elicitation of the biceps reflex.

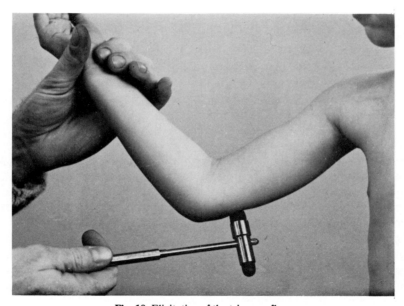

Fig. 10. Elicitation of the triceps reflex.

Response

A quick, slight extension of the elbow caused by contraction of the triceps muscle may be observed.

35

Recording

    0 = absent.

    1 = weak, felt but no seen.

    2 = moderate, visible movement of elbow.

    3 = exaggerated response; clonic beats are only very rarely found; sometimes a slight extension of the fingers.

Threshold of Tendon Reflexes

As each reflex is tested, the intensity of the stimulus in the individually standardized position is varied. If the reflex response is found to be of high intensity or if a weak stimulus is sufficient to elicit the response, the extent of the area from which the reflex is elicitable is explored further.

The examiner faces two main problems: how many trials should be made before the reflex can be considered absent; and which intensity of response out of several trials should be recorded? If no reflex response has been elicited after four or five trials in a good standardized neutral position with stimuli of varying intensity, and the child's muscles are quite relaxed, then a score of 0 can be given. In all cases, at least three immediately comparable responses are required for the eventual score, the stimulus being of equal intensity.

Recording

    0 = no reflex elicitable.

    1 = high threshold, high intensity of stimulus necessary.

    2 = medium threshold.

    3 = low threshold, very low intensity of stimulus necessary; extension of area from which reflex is elicitable.

Significance

Absence or low intensity of reflexes with a high threshold may be a sign of a muscle disease, a peripheral nervous disorder or a lower motor neuron disease. However, in three- and four-year-old children reflexes are rather difficult to elicit and responses are variable. This often bears more relationship to their soma type than to any basic difference in the neuromuscular system at this age.

Exaggerated responses may be due to a lesion of the upper motor neuron. Asymmetries require further investigation, as in combination with other signs they may originate from a hemisyndrome. Obvious asymmetries of tendon reflex responses may sometimes be present as an isolated finding, and they may or may not be of clinical significance. It is possible that one asymmetrical reflex may be the first, or even the only, manifestation of a peripheral nervous disorder or a local muscle disease. It may also be the residual effect of a past disorder (traumata, infectious diseases with high fever, disorders of endocrine gland function).

A high intensity of a reflex is quite often correlated with a low threshold, though this is not inevitable. Children with minor nervous dysfunctions may have a low threshold for a reflex of normal intensity. The reverse may also be found.

Consistent asymmetries in thresholds only and asymmetries without an obvious lateralised pattern may be signs of minor neurological dysfunction. Where laterality is well established (especially in five- to seven-year-old children), a slight asymmetry of the threshold for tendon reflexes may be found but need not be of clinical significance. The low threshold more often occurs on the side of the arm or leg of preference.

The optimal response at all ages for the tendon reflexes and their thresholds is a score of 2, though obviously this does not mean that each non-optimal response is a pathological sign.

Plantar Response (Fig. 11)

Procedure

The examiner holds the child's foot steady in a neutral position and scratches along the lateral side of the sole from the toes towards the heel with the point of a sharp object or his thumbnail. The stimulus should be a firm scratch, but not strong enough to elicit a withdrawal of the leg.

This technique is rather different from the classical test of the plantar response, whereby the examiner scratches along the lateral side of the sole towards the toes. That method has the drawback of terminating with the specific stimulus for the grasp reflex: thus, a plantar flexion of the toes in this instance may indicate either a positive grasp reflex or a plantar response. Clearly, it is important to differentiate between the two, especially as a positive grasp reflex in three- to four-year-old children may be a manifestation of a delay in maturation of the central nervous system.

Response

Three different qualities of response in the big toe may be observed.

(*a*) A negative response; no movement of the toe as a result of the stimulus.

(*b*) A *jerky* dorsi- or plantar flexion of the big toe.

(*c*) A tonic dorsi- or plantar flexion.

In the other toes, spreading or fanning may be present.

Recording

(*a*) *Big toe*

Dorsiflexion:	0 = no reaction.
	1 = jerky dorsiflexion.
	2 = tonic, sustained dorsiflexion.
Plantar flexion:	0 = no reaction.
	1 = jerky plantar flexion.
	2 = tonic, sustained plantar flexion.
(*b*) *Other toes*	0 = no fanning.
	1 = fanning present.

Significance

Although the optimal response is plantar flexion, in clinical practice a 'no reaction' score may also be considered as falling within the optimal range.

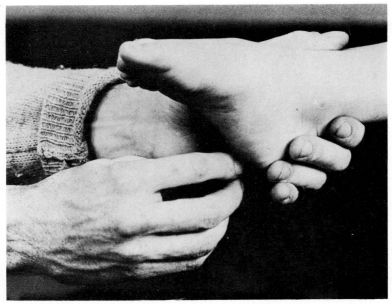

Fig. 11. Elicitation of the plantar response by scratching along the lateral side of the sole from the toes towards the heel.

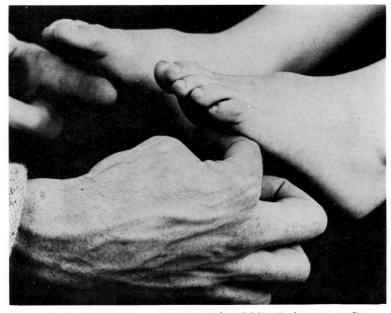

Fig. 12. Position of the examiner's hands for eliciting the foot grasp reflex.

Inconsistent dorsiflexion is frequently seen in children up to the age of four or five. It is usually jerky, but if this jerky dorsiflexion is clearly stereotyped it should be considered abnormal. Variable jerky dorsiflexion may be caused by the child's ticklishness (perhaps a result of tension and nervousness), and is usually of no clinical significance.

Sustained dorsiflexion which does not originate from a foot deformity (pes cavus) reflects a neurological dysfunction, especially if other signs of neurological dysfunction are also present. In the case of pes cavus, the misleading dorsiflexion of the big toe can often be overcome by pushing up the head of the first metatarsal bone. The movement of the big toe (and of the other toes) in the plantar response results from the interplay between foot extensors and flexors. In infants and young toddlers there is a shift of balance between flexors and extensors which favours dorsiflexion and spreading of the toes, whilst in children of three years and over the co-operation between extensors and flexors usually leads to plantar flexion of the toes or an 'indifferent' response (no movement or change of posture whatsoever). When there are foot deformities, the equilibrium between extensors and flexors may again be shifted (for example, towards the dorsiflexed side in pes cavus). Although the disturbance of equilibrium may be overcome by correcting the posture of the foot, the correcting manoeuvre may elicit a grasp response, particularly in toddlers, in which case a clear differentiation of the ultimate movement of the big toe remains problematic. In rare cases, the foot deformity may itself be the result of a neurological disease (*e.g.* Friedreich's or Marie-Hoffman's disease).

Fanning or spreading of the toes is often present in children aged five years or less, but in older children it can be a sign of neurological dysfunction—*i.e.* when it is not part of a general withdrawal movement of the leg.

Asymmetries may be of great significance and require further investigation. Slight differences between the responses of the left and right foot, such as plantar flexion on one side and a negative response on the other, may be regarded as meaningful asymmetries if other slight signs of lateralization are also present. An isolated asymmetry, *i.e.* an asymmetry of the plantar responses without other non-optimal findings, is usually of no clinical significance.

Foot Grasp Reflex (Fig. 12)

Procedure

The examiner places his index finger against the heads of the metatarsal bones, approaching them from the lateral side of the foot, and presses firmly.

Response

Plantar flexion of all toes may be observed.

Recording

    0 = absent.
    1 = weak and unsustained.
    2 = sustained response for approximately 10 seconds.

Significance

A score of 2 is always abnormal. It may be merely a sign of retardation of the nervous system or it may be a manifestation of central nervous system damage. When there is severe deterioration in the functioning of the central nervous system, the grasp reflex may reappear; however, this eventuality surpasses the bounds of minor neurological dysfunction.

A score of 1 is fairly common in children below four years of age and may be of no clinical significance. One must be careful not to confuse the mechanical effect of applying too much pressure to the delicate sole of a child's foot with a reflexogenic plantar flexion of the toes. The latter usually has a short but obvious latency, whilst the first depends purely on the mechanical force.

Ankle Clonus

Procedure

The examiner stabilizes the child's lower leg with one hand while dorsiflexing the child's foot abruptly with his other hand. It is important that the passive stretch which is applied to the foot extension by this manoeuvre is sustained for a few moments. Take care that the ankle joint is fully relaxed, which is most easily obtained when the child's legs and feet hang free. If clonus is present, the passive stretch of extensors should be sustained for as long as the clonus lasts.

Response

When clonus is present, there ensues a series of regularly repeated jerky contractions of the calf muscles. The number of these clonic beats is counted. Both legs are tested.

Recording

    0 = no clonic beats.
    1 = 2-4 clonic beats.
    2 = 5-7 beats.
    3 = 8 beats or more.

Significance

The optimal score for all ages is 0. In cases where the score is the same for both legs, only a score of 3 has any clinical significance, for it may indicate an over-all increased level of muscle reflexes due to a loss of asynchrony in the discharge of motor neurons in the stretch reflexes. This loss of asynchrony may be caused by any supranuclear dysfunction which destroys the inhibitory effect on the segmental stretch reflex. Symmetrical scores of 1 or 2 are usually not significant.

A clonus can be defined as an oscillation of the activity of the muscle spindles during a muscle contraction, so all events which change the equilibrium and adaptability of the equilibrium between intrafusal and extrafusal muscle-fibre activity can lead to a clonus. This happens, for instance, in states of tension or nervousness, which can lead to a non-sustained clonus (score 1 or 2). Sometimes a score of 1 (or even 2) can be found in active boys without obvious tension in the child. Sustained clonus (score 3), however, is always a manifestion of hyperreflexia and indicates damage within the nervous system.

In cases of asymmetrical findings, scores 1 and 2 may also be of clinical significance, as their presence may be part of a mild hemisyndrome.

Palmo-mental Reflex (Fig. 13)

Procedure

Using a fingernail or a pin, the examiner scratches along the radial side of the child's palm and observes the mental muscles of the chin.

Response

A slight, quick contraction of the homolateral musculus mentalis of the chin may be observed. In strong responses, the heterolateral muscle may also show a contraction.

Recording

    0 = absent.

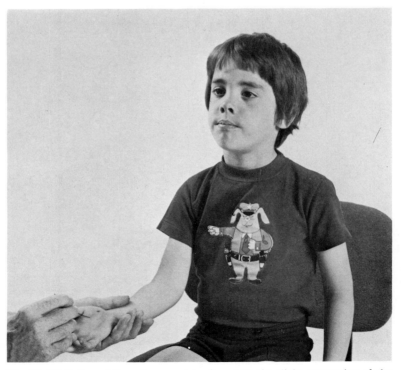

Fig. 13. Elicitation of the palmo-mental reflex; note the slight contraction of the mental muscle.

Fig. 14. Elicitation of the Mayer response.

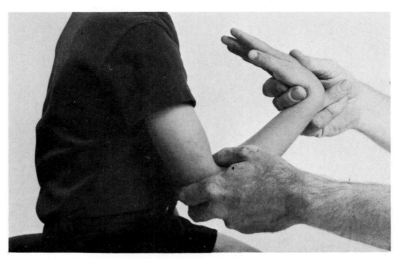

Fig. 15. Elicitation of the Léri response.

42

1 = barely discernible, quick contraction which cannot be reproduced immediately.

2 = obvious contraction on the homolateral side which habituates after two or three trials.

3 = obvious contraction which does not habituate after two or three trials. It often spreads to the heterolateral side, and may even lead to involuntary movement in the peri-oral area.

Significance

The optimal score is probably 0, although a score of 1 is found in many subjects, children as well as adults. A score of 2 is often found in children aged four or less. Older children who show signs of minor neurological dysfunction may have a score of 2. A score of 3 is rare, and is a sign of developmental retardation of the nervous system or of neurological dysfunction.

Mayer and Léri Reflexes (Figs. 14 and 15)

Procedure

The examiner flexes the child's extended fourth finger by pressing it into the palm of the child's hand. This strong passive flexion of the metacarpo-phalangeal joint leads to an adduction and opposition of the extended thumb. This is the Mayer reflex. This manoeuvre can be somewhat painful, so it should be carried out with care in order not to spoil the child's co-operation.

To elicit the Léri reflex, the examiner grasps the child's lower arm with one hand and the child's hand (on the same side) with his other hand. He flexes the child's wrist suddenly and forcefully, and this results in a short-lasting contraction of the elbow flexors.

Recording

0 = absent.

1 = weak response.

2 = evident response.

Significance

These responses are usually present in five-year-olds, but can sometimes be found at earlier ages. They reflect the maturation of the nervous system. Obviously, however, an absence of the response in older children may be due to an upper or lower motor neuron disease or peripheral nerve lesion. Asymmetries can be part of a hemisyndrome, but in five- to six-year-old children the development of laterality must also be taken into account. The responses are often strongest in the preferred hand and arm.

The Mayer and Léri reflexes are normally present. They are associated movements and their appearance is a sign of the differentiation of hand and arm motility.

CHAPTER 6

Assessment of the Child Standing

Behavioural State and Social Responsiveness

The optimal state of the child for the following series of tests is 0, as the results are difficult to interpret if the child is tense or rigid. Social responsiveness can be 0 or 1.

Position

The child should stand up, relaxed and with his arms hanging loosely by his side.

Age

These tests are suitable for all children between three and 12 years of age.

Posture

Procedure

The examiner inspects the posture of the head, body and limbs.

Recording—Head and Trunk

Any persistent deviations from a symmetrical, upright posture are described by noting the appropriate score in the relevant place on the proforma. Special attention should be paid to a deviant posture of the shoulders or pelvis, *i.e.* kyphosis or exaggerated lumbar lordosis. Although these conditions are visible in the fully dressed child, they should be checked again when the child is undressed. A slight scoliosis can go unnoticed while the child is dressed, and the posture of the back must therefore be re-checked at a later stage in the examination (see Abdominal Skin Reflex, p. 82 and Galant Response, p. 84).

Significance

There is often a marked variation in body posture (Figs. 16-17). Round shoulders are often of no neurological significance. A kyphosis and exaggerated lumbar lordosis can result from static defects or from a generalized muscular hypotonia (except in the

---

Captions to Figs. 16 and 17 on facing page:

Fig. 16 (top). A three-year-old child (left) stands broad-based in a rather 'plump' fashion; (centre) the healthy five-year-old can hold his body straight, his base is narrower and the 'plump' posture of the three-year-old has disappeared; (right) the same child seen from the side.

Fig. 17 (below). Standing posture of a slender seven-year-old girl (left) with no neurological abnormalities; note the kyphosis and lumbar lordosis. The same girl after being asked to straighten her back (right); note the exaggerated lumbar lordosis.

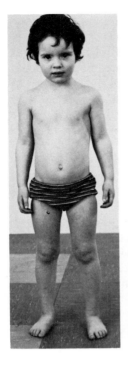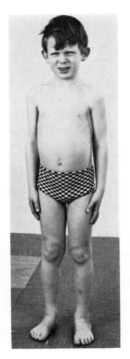

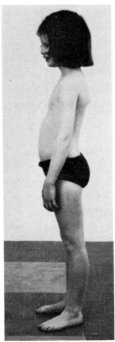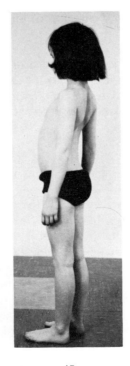

Figs. 16 and 17.
Standing posture at different ages.

45

case of slender young girls, who often show exaggerated lumbar lordosis without any neurological defect).

An asymmetry may be part of a hemisyndrome involving the trunk and/or extremities. In the case of scoliosis, a skeletal anomaly should be suspected, though it may originate from a unilateral muscular weakness (poliomyelitis) or from hypertonia (irritative processes, myositis, intercostal neuritis, renal neoplasm). A paediatric examination is often necessary to exclude the possibility of internal diseases. There is a possibility that, in very rare cases, scoliosis may be one of the first manifest signs of Friedreich's ataxia.

Recording—Upper Limbs

The posture of the freely-hanging arms is described by noting the appropriate score in the relevant box on the proforma. Exorotation, endorotation, flexion, extension, adduction and abduction are scored on a scale ranging from 0 to 2. 0 indicates that the description is not valid, 2 that the description is manifestly valid. Each side of the body is scored separately on the corresponding side of the proforma, so that both symmetrical and asymmetrical deviations can be described. In normal posture, the arms are loosely extended and slightly adducted.

Significance

An asymmetry may be part of a hemisyndrome involving the upper extremities only or the whole body. It may originate from hypertonia or hypotonia. Hypotonia may be due to a peripheral lesion (*e.g.* a plexus paresis), muscle diseases or a dysfunction of the upper motor neurons. Static abnormalities must be excluded.

Recording—Lower Limbs

The posture of the legs and feet is recorded on the proforma, each side being scored separately so that both symmetrical and asymmetrical deviations can be described. Special attention should be paid to the width between the feet required for standing with good balance. The symmetry of the arches of the feet is also inspected and recorded.

Significance

Some degree of genu valgum and pes valgus under six years is usual, and is accompanied by walking and standing on the instep of the foot. The child may thus give the impression of being flat-footed, but if the ankle joint is corrected, the arch often turns out to be sufficient (Figs. 18 and 19). Normal children may vary greatly in this respect, due to the laxity of the ligaments of the joints. Extreme genu valgum and/or pes valgus may sometimes have a neurological cause (hypotonia), especially in children older than about six years. It is essential to differentiate between flat feet (pes planus) and standing on the instep (associated with broad forefeet). The latter is often a sign of hypotonia, whereas flat feet are usually of no neurological significance.

Asymmetries are generally more significant and may be due to static or neurological causes. Accidents resulting in a fractured lower leg or a sprained ankle may lead to a slight asymmetry in posture long after recovery. An asymmetry may also

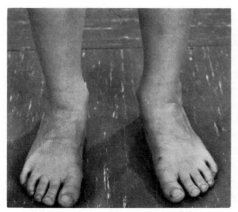

Fig. 18. The feet of a five-year-old child standing on his instep. The arch of the foot appears to be absent. After correction of the posture of the ankle joint, the arch seemed to be adequate.

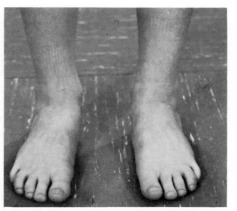

Fig. 19. Flat feet in an eight-year-old child with no neurological abnormalities. After correction of the posture of the ankle joint, the arch of the foot remained inadequate.

be part of a hemisyndrome. Peripheral nervous disorder may be the cause of a unilateral collapsed arch and deviant foot posture. An abnormally large distance between the ankles may be a sign of cerebellar or sensory dysfunction.

An extensive discussion of pes cavus and other foot deformities which accompany severe neurological diseases falls outside the scope of this book. It is well known that pes cavus may be one (or even the only) manifestation of a status dysraphicus, and on rare occasions it may be the first sign of Friedreich's ataxia.

Spontaneous Motility

Procedure

Spontaneous motor activity is observed in the same way as it was in the sitting position (see page 17). A distinction is made between gross and small motor movements, and the quantity and quality of each type of movement are recorded separately. Special attention should be paid to the occurrence of involuntary movements (see page 53).

As the child is at this point standing and waiting for things to happen, it may be difficult to assess the quality of movement. However, during the observation of posture the child may be asked to stand up straight, relax, turn around, *etc.,* and the movements needed for these actions can then be observed for their quality.

Observation of motor activity in the standing position is principally concerned with gross movements, while observation in the sitting position is also concerned with minor movements such as playing with and manipulating toys.

Recording

(a) *Quantity*

Gross movements: 0 = no movements. The child stands perfectly still for at least two minutes.

1 = a few movements only. The child stays in the same place but turns around slightly, shifts his feet and moves his arms, etc.

2 = a moderate amount of movements. The child still stays in more or less the same place, but turns around, bends down, then straightens up again, turns his head around several times, moves his arms, etc.

3 = an excessive amount of movements. The child cannot stay in the same place and continuously moves his body, head and/or limbs.

Small movements: 0 = no movements. The child stands perfectly still without moving hands, feet or facial musculature.

1 = a few movements only, mainly of the hands and face.

2 = a moderate amount of movements. The child opens and closes his hands, pulls faces from time to time wiggles his toes, fidgets with his clothes, etc.

3 = an excessive amount of movements. The child moves and fidgets all the time, makes faces and plucks at his clothes continuously.

(b) *Quality*

Speed: 0 = the child stands perfectly still.

1 = the movements are performed slowly.

2 = the movements are performed at a moderate tempo.

3 = all movements are performed very rapidly.

Smoothness: 0 = the child stands perfectly still.

1 = all movements are very smooth and supple.

2 = movements are mostly smooth and supple, often depending on their speed.

3 = movements are performed clumsily and may be abrupt and jerky, often giving the impression of being broken down into constituent parts.

4 = all movements are performed very awkwardly or are very abrupt and jerky.

Adequacy: 0 = the child stands perfectly still.

1 = movements are easily goal-directed.

2 = some movements are goal-directed, others are inadequate and do not serve a clear purpose.

3 = the child moves around aimlessly; his movements are mainly inadequate.

48

(c) *Involuntary movements*
    Type and localisation are described if present (see page 53).

Significance
    A score of 3 for the quantity of movements denotes overactivity, but such a description does not indicate a diagnosis. Some children may be hyperactive during certain parts of the examination and quiet and attentive for the rest of the time. Others may be active all the time, and in these cases an observation of the quality of movements may well indicate a rather abrupt and jerky motion. We feel that children with very jerky movements are often those with a hyperkinetic syndrome associated with true cerebral dysfunction, whilst children whose hyperactivity is an environmental phenomenon show movements of a different quality.
    Although the quantity of movement is of little diagnostic value in the neurological diagnosis, an accurate observation of the quality of movement of a relaxed and co-operative child may help to detect abnormal motility, and this can then be confirmed or refuted during one of the more specific tests which follow. Signs of neurological dysfunction (*e.g.* dyskinesia, inco-ordination or lack of fine manipulative skills) or a high degree of associated movements which are not age-specific may be seen. Children with inadequate motor control, when performing difficult tasks, often tend to keep their elbow against the trunk—even though they have reached the age when this movement should have disappeared. In addition, they show little spontaneous movement, and their movements in general are fairly slow. This is particularly true of children under six. In older children the movements may seem to be faster, but in fact the movements are broken down into their constituent parts, and this gives the performance a jerky and clumsy appearance.

Posture with Arms Extended (Figs. 20 and 21)

Procedure
    The child is asked to stand with his feet together and his head centred, and then to stretch out his arms, palms downward, for 20 seconds. The test is repeated with the palms turned upward (supination). If possible, the test should be performed with eyes closed so as to avoid a visual correction of the posture of the arms. The hands must be kept slightly apart from each other.

Recording
    Lateral and vertical deviations from the median line are recorded. The degree of pronation which occurs after the hands have been held in supination for some time is also recorded.
    The posture of the wrist joints should be noted, as the hand and forearm are often imperfectly aligned. There may be a kind of double angle, with the wrist being somewhat flexed and the fingers hyperextended in the metacarpal phalangeal joints. This is known as fork-posture or 'spooning'.
    Deviation from horizontal line: 0 = no deviation.
                                          1 = arms drop.
                                          2 = arms rise.

49

Deviation from the median line: 0 = no deviation.
                                                             1 = 30° to 60° sideward.
                                                             2 = 60° to 90° sideward.

Spooning: 0 = no spooning.
                                                             1 = minimal spooning.
                                                             2 = obvious spooning.

Pronation: 0 = no pronation.
                                                             1 = pronation 30° to 60°.
                                                             2 = pronation 60° to 90°.

Each side is scored separately.

Significance

A slight horizontal deviation is fairly common in children below six years of age. The deviation is usually in an upward direction when the arms are pronated and in a downward direction during supination (Figs. 22 and 23). Children of this age group may also show a slight deviation from the median line, and in three-year-olds this is often up to score 1 (Fig. 23). However, all such deviations are abnormal in children of six years and over, and are usually due to hypotonia where the child may over-correct the position of the arms, which may cause him to keep the arms below the horizontal (in pronation) or to bring the hands together in the midline (during

Fig. 20 (*left*). Standing with arms extended and pronated.
Fig. 21 (*right*). Standing with arms extended and supinated.

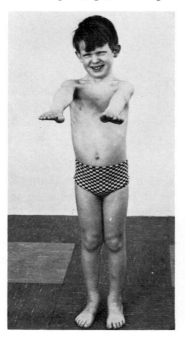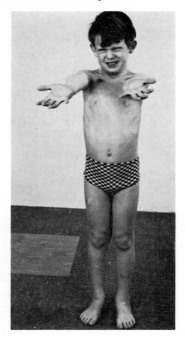

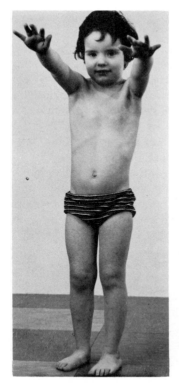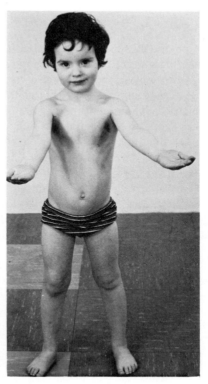

Fig. 22 (*left*). A normal three-year-old girl standing with arms extended and pronated. Note the upward deviation of the arms. A slight deviation to the side is also present.
Fig. 23 (*left*). The same child standing with arms extended and supinated. There is now a downward deviation and again a slight deviation to the side.

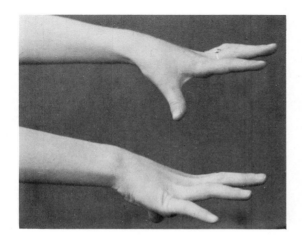

Fig. 24. 'Spooning' of the wrists and hands in a five-year-old girl. When the arms are extended, the wrist joints are slightly flexed and the fingers hyperextended in the metacarpophalangeal joints.

supination). As the eyes are closed during this test, these are purely proprioceptive effects.

Some degree of spooning is common, generally in both arms, and is usually accompanied by a slightly increased range of movement in the wrist and finger joints (Fig. 24). A score of 1 for pronation of outstretched supinated arms is common in children aged less than five years, though three-and four-year old children may not do this test reliably. Spooning of the wrist and hands should be interpreted carefully, as it could be a symptom of hypotonia as well as an inter-individual highly variable laxity of the joints of the fingers and wrist. One should also keep in mind that the ability to show spooning may be merely the result of training.

Asymmetries may be the result of a hemisyndrome or some other unilateral functional disturbance, *e.g.* sensorimotor innervation disturbance, unilateral co-ordination difficulties or local disorders (post-traumatic residual state, muscle or joint diseases, etc.). However, a strongly expressed hand dominance may also account for slight asymmetries, usually in the non-dominant hand.

TESTS FOR INVOLUNTARY MOVEMENTS

Behavioural State and Social Responsiveness

These tests can only be carried out if the child's state is 0.

Fig. 25. Posture for tests of involuntary movements in older children.

Age
These tests are difficult to carry out on children aged less than four.

Procedure
The child is asked to stand with his feet together and his head centred, and then to stretch out his arms with his fingers spread as wide apart as possible, keeping them still for 20 seconds (Fig. 25). Children aged six and over are asked to close their eyes tightly and to stick out their tongue; younger childen may be allowed to keep their eyes open, as they are easily frightened when their eyes are closed. The test must be standardized for age, so that comparisons between the same age-groups can be made.

It is important that the child should put the maximum effort into spreading his fingers as wide as possible, as slight involuntary movements can often only be seen in this position.

General Remarks
The words athetoid and athetotic are extremely misleading; sometimes they are used synonymously and sometimes they are attributed distinct meanings. We have attempted here to give a precise operational definition of what we understand by certain terms in every instance. Where more than one term is used synonymously in the literature we have listed the alternatives but feel that many authors are imprecise in their use of such terms. The fact that one type of movement shows some resemblance to another type of movement does not mean that both types of movement are aetiologically or pathogenetically identical *e.g.* choreatic and choreiform movements.

Choreiform Movements (choreatiform movements)

These are small, jerky movements which occur quite irregularly and arhythmically in different muscles. They may occur in all muscles of the body and can be recorded electromyographically in relaxed muscles when they are not visible on gross inspection.

The examiner should look for choreiform movements in fingers, wrist joints (distal choreiform movements) and in the arms and shoulders (proximal choreiform movements) (Prechtl and Stemmer 1962).

Recording
    0 = no choreiform movements visible during the 20 seconds.
    1 = 2-5 isolated twitches.
    2 = 6-10 twitches, usually in bursts.
    3 = continuous twitching.
Distal and proximal choreiform movements are recorded separately.

Athetotiform Movements (athetoid-like movements)

These are small slow movements, rather writhing in appearance, which occur quite irregularly and arhythmically in different muscles. Presumably, they may occur in all muscles of the body, but are seen most easily in the muscles of the fingers and tongue.

In this test, the examiner should look for athetotiform movements in the fingers only.

Recording
    0 = no athetotiform movements visible during the 20 seconds.
    1 = 2-5 slow writhing movements.
    2 = 6-10 slow writhing movements.
    3 = continuous writhing movements.

Choreo-athetotic Movements

These are usually associated with severe neurological diseases, but they are described here because of the difficulty of distinguishing them, when they are of light intensity, from less marked movements such as choreiform and athetotiform movements.

Choreatic Movements (movements of chorea)

These consist of rather gross, jerky movements occurring irregularly and arhythmically in different muscles. The patient may sometimes have difficulty in keeping his balance because of their amplitude and intensity. The bursts are longer and more gross in comparison with choreiform movements. Electromyographically, choreiform movements appear as short twitches, whilst choreatic movements appear as bursts of activity.

Athetoid Movements (athetotic movements)

These are slow, writhing movements which occur continuously, irregularly and arhythmically in different muscles. They are usually of greater amplitude than athetotiform movements and often cause difficulty in balancing.

Athetosis and chorea are often present at the same time. In athetotic cerebral palsy resulting from kernicterus, athetosis is rarely present without chorea.

Recording
Choreatic movements: 0 = no choreatic movements.
                                 1 = slight choreatic movements which may interfere with ordinary motor activity or posture.
                                 2 = marked choreatic movements which seriously interfere with ordinary activities and occasionally throw the child off balance.
                                 3 = severe choreatic movements which render ordinary activities and normal posture quite impossible.
Athetoid movements: 0 = no athetoid movements.
                                 1 = slight athetoid movements which may interfere with ordinary activities, but not conspicuously.
                                 2 = marked athetoid movements, often in bursts, which seriously interfere with normal motor behaviour.

> 3 = severe athetoid movements which render ordinary
> activities and normal posture quite impossible.

A score of 3 for choreiform movements may resemble a score of 1 for choreatic movements. However this does not mean that choreiform movements can be considered simply as a minor degree of choreo-athetosis.

Tremor

This consists of involuntary, rhythmical, alternating movements.

A clear distinction must be drawn between a resting tremor and a tremor which occurs during movement. In this test, the examiner should look for resting tremor only, in the fingers and forearms.

It is worth noting the frequency and regularity of the tremor. Fast and very regular oscillations of small amplitude are usually of minimal clinical significance, and may be caused by nervous tension. Rarely, such a tremor is based on a familial condition known as 'benign essential tremor'. When there is an association with (often slight) myoclonic jerks, the rare diagnosis of paramyoclonus multiplex must be considered, and in this case the tremor is usually slightly more coarse. A non-essential tremor usually shows less regularity in its frequency and amplitude, particularly during movement.

Recording
> 0 = no tremor present.
> 1 = barely discernible tremor.
> 2 = marked tremor of the fingers.
> 3 = marked tremor of the fingers and arms.

Significance

The significance of choreiform movements is still open to discussion (Rutter *et al.* 1966). However, this type of dyskinesia (Prechtl and Stemmer 1962) seems to be associated with groups of children showing different behaviour (Wolff and Hurwitz 1966) and may be seen as a sign of non-optimal neurological function. Children who do not show choreiform movements at an early age may develop them when they reach the age of four or five; thus, all children in the age group under discussion should be carefully observed for such movements. Once they have emerged, they usually remain until after puberty, when they tend to decrease in intensity and amplitude (Stemmer 1964). Choreiform movements are often associated with slight problems of co-ordination and fine manipulative ability. Obviously, severe choreiform dyskinesia will hamper smooth co-ordination, but inco-ordination and fine manipulative difficulties can also occur when the choreiform movements are very mild, and in such cases the inco-ordination cannot be explained on the basis of the choreiformity alone. This combination is often found in children with behavioural and learning difficulties who also show signs of minor neurological dysfunction.

The incidence of choreiform movements is two to three times higher in boys than in girls, though this sex difference is not so marked for athetotiform movements (the significance of which is also less certain). Athetotiform movements are common in children below five years of age, but they wane with increasing age. They are less commonly associated with co-ordination difficulties and/or problems of fine manipulation. If they persist after the age of five years, they can be considered to be a sign of maturational delay of the nervous system.

Tremor is often seen in children of school age, and often appears to be related to a specific situation. However, some types of tremor are of primary neurological origin (paresis, hereditary tremor) or of secondary neurological origin (thyrotoxicosis, intoxications). A Parkinson-type tremor is rarely found in children and its presence would clearly transgress the bounds of minor dysfunction.

TESTS FOR CO-ORDINATION AND ASSOCIATED MOVEMENTS
Mouth-opening and Finger-spreading Phenomenon (Figs. 26 and 27)

Age

This test is suitable for all children between the ages of three and 12 years.

Procedure

The examiner grasps the child's wrists between his thumb and index finger. He extends the child's arms passively and makes sure that the child relaxes his wrist and finger joints so that the hands hang down loosely. The examiner then asks the child to open his mouth as wide as he can (phase 1), then to close his eyes tightly (phase 2), and finally to stick out his tongue as far as he can (phase 3). Phases 2 and 3 serve to reinforce phase 1.

Response

A spreading and extension of the fingers and thumb is observed, sometimes accompanied by an extension of the joints of the wrist (especially during phases 2 and 3).

Recording

> 0 = no movements of the relaxed fingers and wrists.
> 1 = a barely discernible spreading of the fingers.
> 2 = a marked spreading of the fingers, with some extension.
> 3 = maximal spreading and marked extension of the fingers, often accompanied by extension of the wrists.

A score is given for each phase of the test; the final result consists of the sum of the separate scores (a maximum score of 9 for each hand). Each hand is scored separately.

Significance

This phenomenon is usually present in three- to four-year-olds. It decreases in intensity with age, so that by the age of seven or eight most children show little or no sign of the phenomenon. The persistence of the response in children over eight years of age is a sign of retardation of nervous function. The development of laterality can influence test results in that the mouth-opening and finger-spreading persists for a longer time in the non-preferred hand.

56

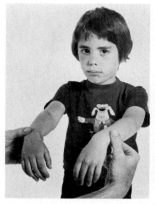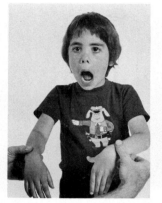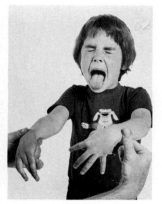

Fig. 26. Initial position of the mouth-opening finger-spreading phenomenon.
Fig. 27a (*centre*). Mouth opening; some extension of the fingers visible.
Fig. 27b (*right*). Tight closing of the eyes; full response, especially on the left.

Diadochokinesis and Associated Movements (Figs. 28 and 29)

Procedure

The child is required to stand with one arm relaxed at his side and the other flexed at an angle of over 90° at the elbow, the hand pointing forwards. The child's head must be centred and his arm and shoulder relaxed. Diadochokinesis consists of quickly pronating and supinating the hand and forearm. The examiner must demonstrate the movement at a speed of four complete pronations and supinations per second. He then asks the child to imitate this movement at the same speed while trying to keep his elbow still and away from his body. Abduction and adduction of the arm often occurs in children, resulting in movements of the elbow. The distance the elbow moves can be used as a measure for the diadochokinesis. The pronating and supinating movements should be smooth and continuous, with no conspicuous pauses at the extreme pronated and supinated positions of the hand. Pauses which occur at the pronated and supinated hand positions should be noted, as they may indicate the presence of a slight disdiadochokinesis.

Associated movements should be looked for in the opposite arm. These consist mainly of mirror movements, sometimes accompanied by flexion of the elbow.

The test lasts approximately 15 seconds.

Recording

Diadochokinesis:　　0 = no pronation or supination of the forearm, but other movements present.

1 = awkward pronation and supination, the elbow moving over a distance of more than 15cm.

2 = awkward pronation and supination, the elbow moving over a distance of 5-15cm.

57

Fig. 28. Diadochokinesis of the right lower arm. On supination of the right hand, associated supination occurs in the left hand.

Fig. 29. On pronation of the right hand, associated pronation occurs in the left hand. Movement of the right elbow during the diadochokinesis is clearly visible (compare with Fig. 28).

	3 = smooth and correctly performed pronation and supination, the elbow moving over a distance of less than 5cm.
Associated movements:	0 = no visible mirror movements or flexion of the elbow.
	1 = barely discernible mirror movements or slight flexion of the elbow without mirror movements.
	2 = marked mirror movements without flexion of the elbow.
	3 = marked mirror movements with flexion of the elbow.

The score for each arm is recorded separately.

Significance

A score of 1 or 2 for diadochokinesis and 2 or 3 for associated movements is quite common in very young children. At the age of six and seven years, the usual score is 2 in both instances, while at the age of eight and over pronation and supination of the forearm is generally smooth and accompanied by a decreasing amount of associated movements. Sometimes at this age a flexion of the elbow may be seen in the opposite arm without any mirror movements in the hand.

Attention should be paid to the tendency to support the elbow against the body, as this may hide an inability to keep the elbow still. Three-year-olds can rotate the forearm and hand only by abducting and adducting the shoulders. There is virtually no pronation or supination of the wrist or forearm. At the age when differentiated lower-arm rotation is still imperfect, the above-mentioned tendency to put the elbow against the body to keep it still is often observed (*i.e.* between the ages of seven and nine years). A well-established agonist/antagonist co-operation reflecting cerebellar mechanisms has already developed, and is shown in the smooth, consecutive motor pattern of the shoulder movements of the three-year-old. Of course, this is a sensorimotor property as well, and is based on intact afferent proprioceptive and efferent motor tracts.

In the case of an intact sensorimotor system and smooth movement patterns during this test (no obvious pauses at the end of a single movement), the elbow movements reflect the degree of maturation of differentiated arm and hand motility, and the presence of pauses (*i.e.* an awkward performance which seems to be broken down into its constituent parts) may reflect a cerebellar dysfunction. It must be kept in mind that such a dysfunction may be accompanied by diffuse hypotonia, with the cerebellum regulating gamma tone to a certain extent, but that non-cerebellar hypotonia can be accompanied by a somewhat clumsy diadochokinesia, with a tendency to support the elbow against the body.

If this test is carried out when the child is sitting down, mirror movements in the legs and feet may also be observed. However, since it is difficult for a single observer to score all these at the same time, and since hand and arm movements are best observed when the child is standing, we decided to concentrate on associated movements in the upper limbs. Quite often an asymmetry between the diadochokinesis and the associated movements on the two sides of the body may be observed. Such a discrepancy between the functioning of the right and left arm often increases with age, the pronation and supination improving at a faster rate on the dominant side. Similarly, the amount of associated movements may decrease at different rates on the two sides as the child grows older. In a child with a clearly established laterality, associated movements may occur on the preferred side when the non-preferred arm is moving. However, when laterality is not so firmly established, associated movements may sometimes be seen to a greater degree in the non-preferred arm.

The appearance of associated movements is also governed by other factors such as stress. The order in which the hands are tested may influence the results, and the effects of learning and practice of skilled and complex movements are uncertain. It is advisable to carry out a preliminary trial for 15 seconds to acquaint the child with the test, and to record his scores on his second attempt.

An asymmetrical performance may be interpreted as an indication of laterality or of a hemisyndrome only if other neurological test items corroborate such an interpretation.

A low score for diadochokinesis and a high score for associated movements in children aged 10 and over may be seen as a sign of retarded maturation of these nervous functions.

Finger-nose Test (Figs. 30 and 31)

Age

This test is routinely appropriate only for children aged four years and over, as the results depend greatly on the child's degree of co-operation. It is often suggested that the finger-nose test can be replaced by asking the child to put his finger on, say, a doll's nose. However, this alternative is, in part, another test, and is quite different

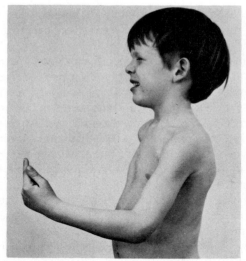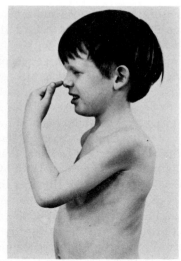

Figure 30 (*left*). The child moves his index finger to his nose, keeping his eyes closed.
Fig. 31 (*right*). He keeps his fingertip on the tip of his nose for a few moments before reopening his eyes.

from visual guiding and other sensory capacities such as the ability to feel the position of one's own nose.

In all the tests that follow, the examiner must be sure that the child understands clearly what he has to do. The child's ability to understand the instructions will depend, obviously, on his intelligence and also on his body schema (knowledge and recognition of parts of one's own body).

Procedure

The child is asked to put the tip of his index-finger (distal finger pulpa) on the tip of his nose. The movement must be carried out slowly. The test is repeated three times with each hand. Children aged five are asked to repeat the test with their eyes closed, but this can upset younger children. The clinical significance and interpretation of the results of this test are greatly influenced by whether the eyes are open or closed during its performance, because of the presence or absence of visual guiding. Therefore, if the child is sufficiently co-operative, one should always ask him to perform the test with eyes closed.

The examiner must demonstrate the test as he gives the instructions. Some children persist in putting their finger on the side of their nose, or touching the bridge of the nose; in these cases, the examiner may take hold of the child's finger and place it correctly on the child's nose, so that the child understands what he is required to do. Sometimes, though rarely, the test must be turned into a game as with a doll ('touch the doll's nose, touch your own nose'), but this should not be necessary if the examiner has established a good relationship with the child.

Recording

The test is scored twice, once for the quality, *i.e.* the smoothness of the movements and signs of intention tremor, and once for adequacy, *i.e.* success in placing the finger tip on the tip of the nose.

Smoothness: 0 = no tremor present during the movement.

1 = slight tremor, occurring only at the end of the movement.

2 = marked tremor, increasing towards the end of the movement.

Tremor is defined here as an oscillating movement of the finger, sometimes of the whole hand, occurring during the movement of the arm. It may be quite irregular and arythmical.

Adequacy: 0 = the child puts his fingertip correctly on the tip of his nose each time.

1 = the child misses the tip of his nose once or twice.

2 = the child misses the tip of his nose each time.

Consistent deviations or misplacings to one side are also described.

Significance

The optimal score for all children over the age of five years is 0. In four-year-olds, smoothness should score 0 and adequacy may score 1. In still younger children, with visual guiding, smoothness and adequacy should score 0, though a score of 1 is still normal, albeit non-optimal.

When the test is performed with eyes closed, it is a test of cerebellar function, though obviously the sensory system (*i.e.* proprioceptors) is also involved. The results of other tests (*e.g.* examination of the sensorimotor system) will help to differentiate between cerebellar and sensorimotor origin in cases of non-optimal performance. If the child keeps his eyes open, visual guidance of the movements provides additional information which is often essential for children aged less than five (Figs. 32 and 33). The need for visual guiding in co-operative children of six years or older may be a sign of developmental delay in cerebellar functioning when there are no other signs of sensorimotor dysfunction. Three-year-olds usually need elbow support against the body in addition to visual guiding (Figs. 32 and 33), but the five-year-old needs neither (Figs. 30 and 31). The need for elbow support in the five-year-old can be considered to be a maturational delay, a delay of differentiated arm motility, or it can be a sign of a slight hypotonia.

Slight difficulties in performing the test (indicated by scores of 1) presumably reflect proprioceptive functions rather than cerebellar functions. However, there is a possibility that they are the first manifestations of a progressive cerebellar disease.

Fingertip-touching Test (Figs. 34 and 35)

Age

This test is suitable for all children between the ages of three and 12 years, but it can only be performed by children of six years and over with the eyes closed.

61

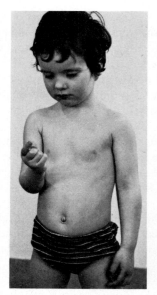

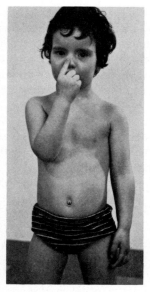

Fig. 32. The finger-nose test in a co-operative three-year-old girl. Visual guidance of the finger movement is necessary.

Fig. 33. Visual guidance is no longer necessary when the goal has been achieved. Note the difference in arm posture compared with Fig. 31; the younger child needs to hold her arm against her body for stabilisation.

Fig. 34. Training procedure for the finger-tip-touching test in a seven-year-old girl; the eyes are open.

Fig. 35. Response with eyes closed in the same girl.

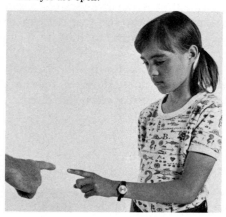

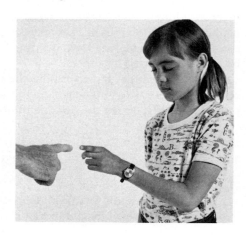

Procedure

The examiner stands in front of the child and points an index finger at him, keeping his elbow flexed. The child is asked to put the tip of his index finger on the tip of the examiner's finger, the distance between them being such that the child has to flex his elbow to accomplish this. The test is carried out three times with each hand, first with eyes open and then with eyes closed. The examiner must take care not to change the position of his finger.

Recording

The test is scored for quality, *i.e.* intention tremor during movement and when the finger is placed, and adequacy, *i.e.* success in placing the fingertip on the examiner's finger. Separate recordings are made when the eyes are open and when the eyes are closed.

Tremor during movement: 0 = no tremor present.
                                   1 = slight tremor.
                                   2 = marked tremor.
Tremor of the placed finger: 0 = no tremor present.
                                   1 = slight tremor.
                                   2 = marked tremor.
Placing the finger: 0 = the child places his finger correctly on the examiner's fingertip each time.
                                   1 = the child misses once or twice.
                                   2 = the child misses each time.
Consistent deviations and misplacings to one side are also described.

Significance

The optimal response (score 0) consists of the child placing his finger smoothly and adequately on the examiner's fingertip. When done with the eyes open, visual guiding plays a preponderant rôle, and, as such, the test gives some general information about hand-eye co-ordination. When carried out with the eyes closed, cerebellar and proprioceptive systems are preponderant for the performance. Generally speaking, the presence of a tremor denotes cerebellar dysfunction, whilst deviations of placing reflect sensory proprioceptive dysfunction. Deviations which occur persistently to one side may be cerebellar or vestibular in origin; in young children (*e.g.* five- or six-year-olds), a score of 2 for placing the finger with no constant deviation toward one side may also reflect a maturational delay of cerebellar functions. Non-cerebellar hypotonia is of course excluded. A score of 1 in placing the finger with eyes closed is normal (albeit non-optimal) in children up to seven or eight years of age. What has been said about elbow support against the body in the section on the Finger-nose Test also applies for this test.

A regular, rather fine tremor—commonly called 'essential' or 'psychogenic' tremor—may be observed, especially while the child's finger rests on the examiner's finger. The term 'psychogenic' emphasises the need for the child to be in the proper behavioural state, as any tension or nervousness may provoke this type of tremor. It is usually of no clinical significance.

Consistent unilateral deviations to one side may reflect a unilateral cerebellar dysfunction, and if there are consistent deviations to one side in both hands, vestibular dysfunction may be involved as well.

Finger Opposition Test

Age

This test is applicable to most children of six years and older. Some agile five-year-olds are also able to perform it.

Procedure

The examiner demonstrates to the child how to place the fingers of one hand (starting with the index finger) consecutively on the thumb of the same hand in the following sequence: 2, 3, 4, 5, 4, 3, 2, 3, 4, 5, *etc.* The child is asked to imitate these movements, completing five sequences to and fro. Each hand is tested in turn. The test should be carried out at a rate of approximately three to four seconds for one complete sequence.

Recording

This test is scored on three aspects: the smoothness of movement, governed by hesitations in correcting mistakes and associated movements in the other fingers of the same hand; smoothness of transition from one finger to the next, especially at the turning-points involving the index and the little fingers; and mirror movements, *i.e.* associated movements in the opposite hand.

A distinction must be made between a poor performance in the general 'smoothness of movement' (which may include hesitations in correcting mistakes) and a poor performance in the smoothness of the finger-to-finger transition (implying broken movements of a jerky and clumsy character), as the latter fault may point to a lack of cerebellar co-ordination of agonists and antagonists during the single finger movement.

Smoothness of movement:
0 = smooth placing of fingers on the thumb.
1 = the child hesitates, sometimes misplaces a finger, gets the sequence wrong or wiggles a finger before placing it.
2 = many hesitations and misplacings with associated movements of other fingers which hamper adequate placing.

Finger-to-finger transition:
0 = easy and immediate transition.
1 = the child puts the same finger on the thumb several times at the turn.
2 = the child repeatedly puts a finger on the thumb before going on to the next finger.
3 = the child repeatedly puts a finger on the thumb and does not go on to the next finger even when he wants to.

Mirror movements:	0 = no associated movements in the opposite hand.
	1 = barely discernible associated movements.
	2 = marked associated movements.

Significance

Most children aged six and over can perform this test. A score of 0 or 1 for finger-to-finger transition and smoothness of movement is possible in normal eight-year-olds. A score of 1 for mirror movements may be present up to the age of 10 years. Girls usually perform this test better than boys.

This test, and particularly the score for 'smoothness of movement', reflects a complex motor performance which requires a neat differentiation in the use of the intrinsic muscles of the hand and fingers. The cerebral cortex is probably involved to a larger extent in this test than in the earlier less complex tests. This is suggested by the fact that the finger-opposition test may be carried out imperfectly even when the finger-nose test and finger-tip-touching tests are performed adequately. Presumably, the finger-opposition test reflects an aspect of the maturation of the cerebral cortex in instances when the cerebellar and proprioceptive systems are already developed. Naturally, hand preference is an important quality in the factor of the performance. Learning is also important, and it is advisable to let the child practise five sequences before his performance is scored. Young children often have difficulty with this test, so the examiner must make quite sure that the child knows what he has to do before the test begins.

What was said previously about elbow support against the body (p. 61) applies here too, especially with regard to hypotonia.

Some children show mirror movements in the resting hand, and these mirror movements may indicate a retarded maturation of the nervous system. Most children of 10 years and over show no mirror movements, and girls usually show fewer associated movements than boys.

Follow-a-finger Test

Age

This test is suitable for most children of six years of age and over. Some agile five-year-olds can also perform it.

Procedure

The child is asked to keep the tip of his index finger at a distance of 1cm from the examiner's index finger, and to follow the examiner's movements closely. The examiner's hand describes a pattern in various vertical and horizontal directions, with some angles of 90°. Both hands are tested consecutively.

Recording

Attention is paid to the smoothness of movement and to any overshooting during changes in direction of movement.

0 = smooth movement, no overshooting or overshooting less than 3cm.

1 = Slightly hesitant movement; overshooting between 3 and 6cm.
2 = clumsy movement; overshooting over 6cm.

Significance

Following a finger is a complex motor performance involving co-ordination mechanisms of spinal and cerebellar origin as well as cortical mechanisms. The interpretation of the results of this test will depend on the results of other tests which assess cerebellar and dorsal cord functions. (This is also the case with the finger-opposition test, p. 64).

Children of about six years usually score 0 or 1, and from seven years onwards a score of 0 can be expected. Hand preference seems to be involved in the test. Any tremor observed during the performance should be noted; a distinction must be made between a fine, regular oscillation and an intention tremor, which is generally more coarse and of variable frequency and amplitude. It is often difficult to differentiate between tremor and overshooting, especially when the overshooting is less than 3cm (score 0). But we should remember that overshooting occurs at the end of movements, whilst tremors are present during larger parts of the movements or during the whole movement.

What has been said about elbow support against the body for stabilization must be remembered during this test as well.

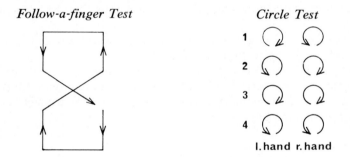

Follow-a-finger Test   *Circle Test*

Circle Test

Age

This test is suitable for most children of six years of age and over. Some agile five-year-olds are also able to perform it.

Procedure

The examiner describes circles in the air with his extended index finger, wrist and forearm (elbows semi-flexed). He makes the movements with both arms simultaneously but in opposite directions. The child is asked to copy the movements. After completing four or five circles, the movement is repeated in the reverse direction. Then, without a pause, the circular movements are made with both arms in the same direction. After completion of about five circles in this way, the direction is reversed.

66

Attention is paid to the ability to copy mirror circles in both directions (to the left and to the right), to the ability to copy uni-directional circles in both directions, and to the transition between the motor patterns of mirroring and uni-directional circling of hands and forearms.

Mirror circles:	0 = perfect circles with both hands and arms.
	1 = different quality of the circles between both hands and arms.
	2 = badly shaped circles or even unrecognizable pattern on both sides (*e.g.* horizontal or vertical swipes or swaying movements).
Unidirectional circles:	0 = perfect circles with both hands and arms.
	1 = different quality of performance between both sides.
	2 = badly shaped circles or even unrecognizable pattern on both sides.
Transition between mirror and unidirectional circles:	0 = immediate and smooth transition.
	1 = hesitation and/or two or three badly-shaped unidirectional circles during transition.
	2 = distorted unidirectional pattern.

Significance

Assuming that co-ordination is intact and well-developed, this test evaluates the co-operation and interplay between the right and left side of the brain. In six-year-old children, and in many five-year-olds, the first part of the test can be carried out easily, mirroring being an easy problem for the brain; but the second part (in which both sides have to be in close interaction as far as time and rhythm are concerned, but in an opposite action regarding the direction of the movement) gives rise to many difficulties. Seven-year-olds can perform both parts, but often have difficulties with the transition, so that they often need a pause between the two parts in order to be able to perform correctly. From the age of eight years onwards, a score of 0 can be expected for both parts of the test and for the transition. Bad scores in this test usually accompany bad scores in the former two tests, and may be interpreted as a developmental retardation of cortical functions—when no other deviant signs indicating sensorimotor dysfunction are present.

Laterality can influence the performance, and six- and seven-year-olds may make better circles with the preferred hand. Elbow support against the body may occur, especially in young and/or hypotonic children.

In children of 10 years of age and over, the test can be done by drawing circles with fingers and wrists only, keeping the elbows still during the performance.

10-year-olds usually still need some co-movement from the elbows, but from 12 years of age onwards an adequate performance may be expected without such co-movements.

Standing with Eyes Closed (Romberg Test)

Procedure

The child is asked to keep his eyes closed for 10 to 15 seconds. With very young children it may be necessary to invent a game, *e.g.* 'Let's see how long you can stand still with your eyes closed. Close your eyes and I shall count how long you can do it'.

Recording

As this is a test of balance, *i.e.* the ability to maintain equilibrium without visual control, the amount of movement of body, arms, legs and feet needed for this purpose is recorded.

      0 = no balance with eyes closed. The child has to move his foot to one side in order to prevent himself from falling.

      1 = balance is only possible with the aid of movements of the whole body, often resulting in a slight shifting of the feet.

      2 = balance is possible with the aid of only a few movements of the ankles and toes.

      3 = perfect balance and no movements.

A consistent tendency to fall to one side is recorded.

Significance

Slight swaying movements of the body unaccompanied by isolated arm or leg movements are often seen, especially at the end of the time limit, and do not seem to have any clinical significance.

Children aged less than six often need a few movements of ankles and toes to maintain balance, without any actual displacement of the feet, and this also appears to be without clinical significance. From the age of seven onwards, one can expect an optimal performance.

Quite often, involuntary movements may interfere with optimal performance and this should be taken into account in the final interpretation of the findings.

A tendency to fall to one side may be a sign of unilateral vestibular or cerebellar dysfunction. A lack of balance without consistent laterality often reflects retardation of balance maturation, a muscular weakness or intensive dyskinesia.

Reaction to Push against the Shoulder during Standing

Age

This test is suitable for all ages, especially if performed in a playful manner.

Procedure

The child is asked to stand upright with his head centred, his arms hanging freely and his feet about 5cm apart. The examiner gives a gentle sideways push against the child's shoulder, the intensity of the push being graded according to the child's age. The child's ability to remain standing without a sideward placing of his contralateral leg is recorded.

Response

The child will try to preserve his balance by shifting his body to the ipsilateral side. If he does not succeed, he may bend to the contralateral side, show some abduction of the arms, and may eventually even side-step to the contralateral side. By keeping his free hand on the contralateral side, at some distance from the child's body, the examiner can prevent the child with poor balance from falling. This gesture also reassures the child, and is very important with very young children.

Recording

      0 = the child falls sideways and has to be caught.
      1 = the child steps sideways.
      2 = the child shows an abduction of the arms at the shoulder.
      3 = the child does not move except for some rapidly checked swaying movements.

Overshooting to the ipsilateral side may sometimes occur, and in this case, side-stepping may occur on that side.

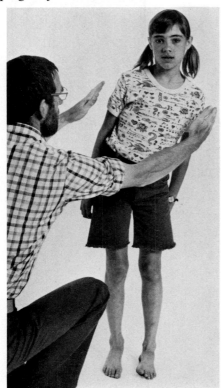

Fig. 36. Response to push against the shoulder in standing position; note the immediate righting reactions of the head.

69

Significance

In children up to six years of age, scores of 2 and 3 are optimal; in older children the optimal score is 3. An inability to perform this test correctly may be caused by poor postural control due to muscle weakness (hypo- or hypertonia), postural abnormalities, or mild disturbances of trunk co-ordination of cerebellar or proprioceptive origin. In the latter case especially, irregular gross oscillations may occur, whilst in slight cerebellar dysfunction a broadening of the standing base seems more obvious.

The test is a refinement of 'Reaction to Push against the shoulder during Sitting' described on p. 21.

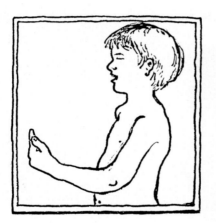 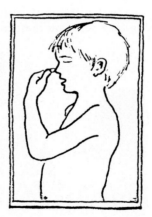

CHAPTER 7

Assessment of the Child Walking

Behavioural State and Social Responsiveness
The optimal state for the following series of tests is 0, though the score for social responsiveness can be 0 or 1.

Position
The child is asked to stand with his head straight and his hands by his sides.

Age
These tests are suitable for all children between three and 12 years of age, except where indicated.

Gait

Procedure
The child is asked to walk approximately 20 continuous paces and back. He should be relaxed and walk quietly at a normal pace. The examiner must look out for 'acting'.

Fig. 36. Walking.

Recording
The posture of the child's head, body and arms while walking is recorded (see scoring criteria, p. 20). Special attention should be paid to the width of the gait, movements of the arms and movements of the hips and knees. If flexion of the hip, knee and/or ankle is impaired on one side, the child will compensate for this by circumducting the leg in an arc away from the hip. (In extreme cases, such as spastic hemiplegia with equinovarus posture of the foot, the pelvis will be raised on the affected side and the toes may still scrape against the floor.) The examiner should also note the way in which the feet are placed: in normal gait the heel touches the ground first and the weight of the body is then shifted to the toes with an arching of the foot.

This is referred to as the 'heel-toe' gait. The position of the feet in relation to the lower leg is described, with special attention being paid to possible valgus postures such as endorotation or exorotation combined with passive pronated position of the foot (walking on the instep).

Asymmetries or other deviations of posture resulting, for instance, from slight scoliosis, slight diffuse hypotonia or asymmetrical, mainly static, foot posture which are present when the child is standing may disappear during walking. The reverse may also happen. These phenomena should be described.

Width of gait:	0 = constant.
	1 = variable.
	0 = <10cm.
	1 = 11-20cm.
	2 = 21-30cm.
	3 = >30cm.
Circumduction:	0 = no circumduction.
	1 = barely discernible (left and/or right).
	2 = marked (left and/or right).
Movements of pelvis:	0 = short abrupt movements.
	1 = swinging movements.
	2 = dipping movements.
Movements of the knees:	0 = alternating flexion/extension.
	1 = constantly flexed.
	2 = constantly extended.
Heel-toe gait:	0 = no heel-toe gait, no arching of the foot.
	1 = heel-toe gait, but no evident arching of the foot.
	2 = heel-toe gait, marked arching of the foot.
Arm movements:	0 = normal swing.
	1 = arms hanging down without any active movement.
	2 = arms kept in abduction.
	3 = arms kept in adduction.
Placing of the feet:	Each foot is scored separately for abduction, adduction, dorsiflexion and plantar flexion on the medial and lateral side.

In difficult cases, Holt's footprint method (1965) may be useful.

Significance

Asymmetries in the posture of the head or body during walking may be due to neurological or orthopaedic causes (*e.g.* hemiplegia or rheumatoid arthritis). In cases of generalised hypotonia, the posture may be symmetrical but abnormal. Asymmetries in arm or leg movements may be signs of a mild lateralisation or hemisyndrome.

Children below the age of six quite often show only minimal arching of the foot, and in extreme cases the foot may even be endorotated and pronated (walking on the instep). Often these children cannot walk long distances and tire easily on walking trips. Generally, no arching of the foot is visible when the child is standing still. A perpendicular from the internal malleolus reaching the floor outside the circumference of the footprint indicates talipes valgus (see Fig. 18, page 47). At this age, this is usually a result of lax ligaments around the ankle joints, and postural deviations generally disappear during the course of the next few years as the ligaments grow stronger. There may be a neurological cause such as hypotonia, but this is rare. Most so-called 'flat feet' at this age are really talipes valgus disorders. Treatment with arch supports (which do not act causally) is of little value; the ideal treatment is the introduction of strong shoes that support the ankle joint and counteract the tendency to walk on the instep. Asymmetries and extreme cases of symmetrical talipes valgus must be carefully examined as they may be of neurological origin (*e.g.* lateralisations, hypotonia, isolated hypertonia).

Children below the age of five tend to show only a few arm movements while walking, the four-year-old generally keeping his arms still.

In children over the age of six, arching of the foot should be evident during walking and should generally be visible during standing. If the posture of the ankle joint is adequate but there is no arching, pes planus should be suspected (see Fig. 19, p. 47). Static or hereditary factors are important in most cases. In cases of marked pes planus, a symmetrical abduction posture of the feet is usual.

Walking on the instep is usually a sign of mild hypotonia in children over six or seven years of age, but it can also be an early sign of progressive muscle weakness.

Circumduction of one leg results from inadequate integration of knee and/or ankle movements in locomotion, and may be due to nervous dysfunction (such as spastic hemiparesis) or to arthrogenic or myogenic causes. In cases of mild hypertonia on one side of the body, circumduction may be evident before the examination of the resistance against passive movements reveals any difference between the two legs. This must be differentiated from the effects of pain which, by immobilising joints, may also lead to some degree of circumduction.

In normal gait, the distance between the feet remains constant. A variable width of gait may be arthrogenic (*e.g.* luxation or subluxation of the hip joint) or neurological in origin, although once again this must be differentiated from a variable width of gait due to pain.

In very young children (two to three years) slight asymmetries of gait may be observed, unaccompanied by other signs of neurological dysfunction. It is possible that in these cases a certain degree of plagiocephaly (asymmetry of the skull, generally the result of postnatal head posture) may be present (Robson 1968). Children of three to four years may also show asymmetries of gait without evidence of other neurological dysfunction. These usually disappear as the child grows older. Arthrogenic or static causes may be found in some of these children, but even if no such causes can be diagnosed, the clinical significance of such an isolated finding is doubtful.

The normal width of gait in children over three years of age is 11 to 20cm. A very narrow gait may result from hypertonia of the adductor muscles of the leg, which, in cases of mild diplegia, can occur without any evidence of scissoring of the legs. A wide gait may be caused by nervous dysfunction (*e.g.* muscular hypotonia of the leg and/or pelvic girdle, sensory or cerebellar dysfunction) or may be arthrogenic in origin, as in the case of luxation or subluxation of the hip joint. Dipping and strong swinging movements of the hips may be caused by muscle diseases (*e.g.* gluteal muscle weakness) or by hip dysplasia, the latter sometimes resulting from hypertonia (*e.g.* spasticity of internal pelvic rotatory muscles and/or leg adductors). However, swinging movements of the hips during walking can also occur in cases of hypotonia and in cases of hypertonia without hip dysplasia. Obviously, hip subluxations independent of neurological disease will lead to distorted hip movements during walking, with a marked dipping of the pelvis with each stride. Children who are accustomed to sitting on the floor between flexed legs may show a gait characterised by a moderate amount of swinging movements of the hips and changing width of gait. This is caused by a lengthening of the abductors and a shortening of the adductors of the upper leg as a result of the sitting posture. This posture is chosen mainly by children who are slightly hypotonic.

It must be borne in mind that the individual's foot postures can vary considerably during walking, and that findings may therefore be rather difficult to interpret. Marked exo- or endorotation or marked dorsi- or plantar flexion should arouse the suspicion of abnormality, as should any obvious asymmetries. However, as with other signs, a final interpretation can only be made when the full examination has been completed.

Walking Along a Straight Line

Age
The test is suitable for children between the ages of five and 12 years.

Procedure
The child is asked to walk along a straight line for approximately 20 continuous paces and then back again. If he is below seven years of age he is not required to place one foot directly in front of the other.

Recording
The number of deviations from the line are counted.
0 = the child deviates from the line continuously. He is unable to take two or three successive steps in a straight line.
1 = more than six deviations.
2 = 4-6 deviations.
3 = 1-3 deviations.
4 = no deviations.

Significance
Walking along a straight line is often difficult before the age of seven years, and some deviations occur even when the child is not required to place one foot directly in front of the other. The optimal response from the age of five years onwards is a score of 4 (remembering that the technique changes when the child reaches the age of seven), but score 3 can be considered normal up to the age of nine years.

Poor performance may be due to hypotonia, hypertonia, cerebellar or sensory dysfunction. Moreover, involuntary movements such as choreiform dyskinesia or tremor (high intensity) may interfere with the child's performance. Persisting deviations to one side may reflect a hemisyndrome of cerebellar or non-cerebellar origin.

Some children place their feet correctly on the straight line but they show many swaying movements of the arms and body. If mild hypotonia and nervous tension are excluded in such cases, the children can be considered to be slow in the development of balance. These children often have difficulty in standing with their eyes closed (Romberg Test), which suggests a vestibular involvement (see page 68).

Walking on Tiptoe (Fig. 38*a*.)
The child is asked to walk on tiptoe for approximately 20 paces and back.

Recording
    0 = unable to walk on tiptoe.
    1 = heel raised for a few moments only.
    2 = the heel remains off the ground.
    3 = the child walks well on tiptoe.

Any head, body or arm movements which are not present in ordinary walking must be recorded as associated movements. (Slight swinging of the arms, for instance, is acceptable.) Associated movements are seen most clearly in the arms and face. Generally, the arms and hands extend and lip and tongue movements may also be present. Clenched fists may be seen, but are considered as associated movements only when they are accompanied by extended arms.
    0 = no associated movements visible.
    1 = barely discernible movements in the arms and hands only.
    2 = marked extension of the arms and hands, or extension of the arms with clenched fists.
    3 = same as '2' above, plus abduction of the upper arms and/or lip and tongue movements.

Significance
Children over three years of age should be able to walk on tiptoe; some younger children are also able to do so, but if they cannot no abnormality is indicated. A poor performance may be due to hypotonia or flexor hypertonia, and a very good performance may be due to extensor hypertonia. Asymmetries may indicate a lateralisation syndrome and should be carefully investigated after having first established that there are no deformities of the feet or other possible non-neurological causes. Mild hemisyndromes may present with walking on tiptoe and on heels before they can be seen in ordinary walking or can be felt while testing the resistance against passive and active movements. Corroboration of the unilateral findings can then usually be obtained by inspecting the sitting posture, standing posture and the posture of legs and feet while the child is lying in prone and supine positions. Bilateral foot deformities may also influence performance.

Associated movements usually decrease with increasing age, and should have

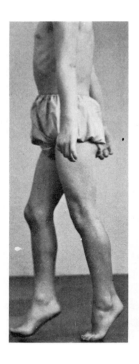

Fig. 38a. Walking on tiptoe. Slight extension of the elbows is present.

Fig. 38b. Walking on heels. Marked associated movements are visible (flexion of the elbow, slight hyperextension of the wrist, extension and spreading of the fingers).

Fig. 39. Standing on the left leg.

Fig. 40. Hopping on the right leg.

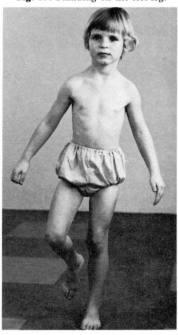
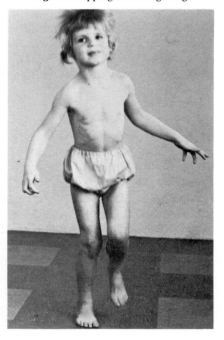

disappeared by the age of seven or eight years. The persistence of associated movements is one possible manifestation of slow neurological development.

Walking on Heels

Procedure

The child is asked to walk on his heels over a distance of approximately 20 paces and back (Fig. 38*b*).

Recording

    0 = unable to walk on heels.
    1 = toes raised for only a few moments.
    2 = toes remain off the ground.
    3 = the child walks well on the dorsal half of the heels.

Any movements of the head, body or arms which are not present in ordinary walking must be recorded as associated movements. Associated movements are seen most clearly in the arms and face: the arms flex at the elbow; the wrists hyperextend and the fingers flex at the interphalangeal joints; the fingers may also be extended. The upper arms are often abducted at the shoulder joint, and lip and/or tongue movements may be observed.

    0 = no associated movements visible.
    1 = barely discernible flexion of the elbows and hyperextension of the wrists.
    2 = marked flexion of the elbows ($\leqslant 60°$) and hyperextension of the wrists.
    3 = as for '2' above (but elbow flexion $\geqslant 60°$ with abduction of the shoulders and/or movements of lips and tongue).

Significance

Children over the age of three years should be able to walk on their heels, and some younger children may also be able to do so. A poor performance may be due to hypotonia of the lower leg muscles or paresis. It is of particular interest to note here that paresis of the peroneal muscles may occur without other muscles being impaired to the same degree. The child will walk on the outer side of the foot rather than on the heels, or, in mild cases, will commence walking on the heel but will fail and soon afterwards will walk on endorotated feet. Mildly hypotonic children who walked on the instep during the test for ordinary walking may show the same phenomenon, with no signs of muscle paresis. Non-hypotonic children who walk on the instep (mainly children under six years of age) usually walk normally on the heels. As already stated in the section on walking on tiptoe (p. 75), the presence of a mild hemisyndrome may be discovered by close inspection of the symmetry of walking on the heels. Clearly, any foot deformities will interfere with performance. Asymmetries may indicate a lateralisation syndrome or they may result from non-neurological causes (*e.g.* unilateral foot deformities, arthrogenic origins).

Associated movements disappear at an earlier age for the test of walking on tiptoe than for walking on heels, but these movements have usually disappeared from the performance of walking on the heels by the age of nine or 10 years. The persistence of associated movements at this age may be interpreted as a sign of slow neurological development.

Standing on One Leg

Procedure

The child is asked to stand on one leg for at least 20 seconds. Each leg is tested in turn, the child being allowed to start with whichever leg he prefers (Fig. 39).

Recording

The performance of each leg is recorded separately and a note is made of which leg the child uses first.

    0 = unable to stand on one leg.
    1 = tries, but has to put foot down again.
    2 = 3-6 secs.
    3 = 7-12 secs.
    4 = 13-16 secs.
    5 = 17-20 secs.
    6 = more than 20 secs. This is regarded as a mature performance.

Swaying or 'balancing' movements are also recorded, and it is noted whether they are abrupt and jerky or continuous.

Significance

The ability to stand on one leg develops quite suddenly and improves rapidly. At three years of age only a few children can stand on one leg for longer than five to six seconds; at five years, most children can carry on for 10 to 12 seconds; at six, 13 to 16 seconds is normal; and by the age of seven or eight, most children are able to stand on one leg for more than 20 seconds.

The difference between the performance of the preferred and the non-preferred leg is greatest at the age of four and five years and decreases with age. At the age of three or four, a difference of 1 or 2 points is not unusual. At this age, many 'balancing' movements are also seen. In children over the age of five or six the amount of 'balancing' decreases and the ability to stand on one leg is similar for each side. The persistence of continuous balancing movements after the age of seven years can be regarded as a sign of slow development of equilibrium.

Sudden jerks which nearly throw the child off balance may be due to involuntary dyskinesia such as proximal choreiform movements.

It should be noted that the preferred leg for standing and hopping is not always the same as the one for kicking a ball for instance. Children under seven or eight years often choose their preferred leg for standing (*i.e.* for stabilisation) and use their non-preferred leg for kicking the ball. The reason is that their balance at this age is still quite poor, and they need the more differentiated leg for this balancing. Children over the age of eight years usually kick the ball with their preferred leg, for at this age they can maintain balance with their non-preferred leg, leaving the preferred leg for more complex tasks such as estimating force and directing the ball.

Asymmetrical performances should be interpreted very carefully. Extreme cases of asymmetry may reflect a lateralisation syndrome, in which case there will undoubtedly be other signs of nervous dysfunction which show an analogous pattern.

Involuntary movements, particularly choreiform movements or tremor, will interfere with the child's performance. A low score for each leg, unaccompanied by dyskinesia, may result from a retardation in functional maturation, from generalised hypotonia or from cerebellar or sensory dysfunction.

Hopping

Procedure

The child is asked to hop on each foot at least 20 times, starting with whichever leg he prefers (Fig. 40). Hopping on the spot is best, but children younger than six often cannot manage this and so should be allowed to move forwards. The child is asked to hop on his toes, and not with the whole foot.

Recording

The performance of each foot is recorded separately, and the preferred leg is recorded.

    0 = unable to hop.
    1 = 2-4 hops.
    2 = 5-8 hops.
    3 = 9-12 hops.
    4 = 13-16 hops.
    5 = 17-20 hops.
    6 = more than 20 hops.

The amount of swaying and balancing movements are noted, as well as the child's ability to remain hopping on his toes. Hopping on the whole foot can be heard as well as seen. Evident asymmetries in arm posture should be recorded.

Significance

The development of this motor function is abrupt and rapid. At three years, very few children are able to hop even a few times, and then it is usually only on one foot; whilst at four years five to eight hops is a normal score. At five years, nine or 10 hops are possible; and at six years between 13 and 16 hops. At six years about 25 per cent of children can hop more than 20 times on one foot at least. At seven or eight years, the majority of children can hop more than 20 times with each foot.

The presence of continuous balancing movements after the age of seven years may reflect a slow development of equilibrium. Abrupt and jerky disturbances of balance may be due to choreiform or some other involuntary dyskinesia.

Children below the age of seven may or may not hop on the whole foot: they may start on tiptoes and then gradually begin to use the whole foot. Hopping on the whole foot in older children usually reflects hypotonia.

Asymmetries in arm posture during hopping may be a sign of a mild lateralisation. Between the ages of five and seven, one leg is often better than the other one, though, as with standing on one leg, the best leg is not necessarily the preferred leg in playing football, for example. The relationship of hopping to the concept of dominance is a complex one; consequently, an asymmetrical performance must be very carefully interpreted. The greater the discrepancy between left and right, the greater the possibility of a hemisyndrome or other lateralisation syndrome as the underlying cause. If such a lateralisation is present, other neurological findings should corroborate it.

A weak performance on both sides may reflect a retardation in maturation; neurogenic, myogenic, static or arthrogenic causes must also be considered. Pain from a different origin may also interfere with performance.

It is possible that training may influence results, but as most children at play hop only on their leg of preference, the training will be asymmetrical. As in the case of other tests such as diadochokinesis and standing on one leg, girls tend to perform better than boys.

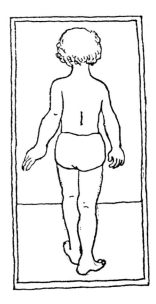

CHAPTER 8

Assessment of the Trunk

Behavioural State and Social Responsiveness
The optimal state and social responsiveness of the child for the following series of tests is 0, though the tests are possible if it is 1.

Position
At this point in the examination, the child should undress to allow inspection of the trunk, and the elicitation of responses such as the abdominal skin and Galant responses. The child should stand relaxed, his feet equidistant from the midline, his head centred and his arms hanging by his side.

Age
These tests are suitable for all children aged three to 12.

Inspection of the Back

Procedure
The examiner should carefully inspect the spine and the skin of the back.

Recording
Any deviations from normal erect posture and any peculiarities of the skin are described. The movements of the spine forward, backward, to the side and in rotation are inspected and described if abnormal. Special attention should now be paid to possible lateral incurvation of the spine (*i.e.* scoliosis), particularly if observation of sitting, standing and walking has already aroused the suspicion of scoliosis.

Significance
Normally the thoracic part of the back is slightly curved forward while the lumbar part shows a certain degree of lordosis; there may be considerable variability between individuals (see Figs. 16 and 17, page 45). A lateral incurvation is always abnormal. In hypotonic children, thoracic kyphosis and lumbar lordosis may be accentuated.

The skin along the midline of the back is worth particularly careful inspection. Naevi, dimples, hairy patches or slight lipomas may be the only external signs of an underlying spina bifida occulta.

Naevi ordered laterally from the midline and often in dermatome areas (café-au-lait spots) or slight fibromas, etc., may arouse the suspicion of Recklinghausen's disease before the appearance of other symptoms. The naevi vasculosi which accompany Sturge-Weber's disease may be present on the skin of the back when they are not very conspicuous in the trigeminal area of the face; more often, they are not confined just to the skin of the back. Café-au-lait spots, combined with white (vitiligo) spots and sebaceous adenomas (often only pin-point size), may be a sign of tuberous sclerosis before the disease is clinically evident. Sometimes sebaceous adenoma is the sole sign, which may be present for many years without other symptomatology.

Any limitation of the movement of the spine should be further explored, especially if corroborated by findings during palpation. It may be of neurological or articular origin. In the case of scoliosis, a skeletal anomaly should be suspected but it may also result from unilateral hyper- or hypotonia, or unilateral irritating processes (see page 46).

SKIN REFLEXES

Abdominal Skin Reflex (Fig. 41)

Procedure

The examiner scratches with a pin from the side of the abdominal wall towards the centre, above, on a level with and below the navel. Obviously the behavioural state and social responsiveness must be 0 for this test. We prefer a standing position, as experience has shown that a lying child tends to contract his abdominal muscles. Sometimes it is worthwhile to distract the child by talking to him or drawing his attention to some surrounding object in order to obtain full relaxation of his abdominal muscles.

Response

There should be a contraction of the abdominal muscles in the stimulated area. In fat children the contraction may be hardly visible (score 1).

Recording
> 0 = absent.
> 1 = weak, just discernible reaction.
> 2 = marked contraction.

Cremasteric Reflex (Figs. 42 and 43)

Procedure

The examiner takes a pin and scratches down the inner side of the upper leg.

Response

There should be a quick elevation of the testis; a bilateral response may be obtained. If there is no response the examiner should ascertain whether the testicles are descended into the scrotum.

Recording
> 0 = absent.
> 1 = weak, barely discernible elevation of the testis.
> 2 = marked elevation of the testis.

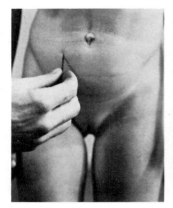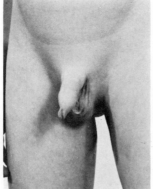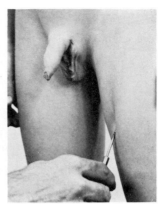

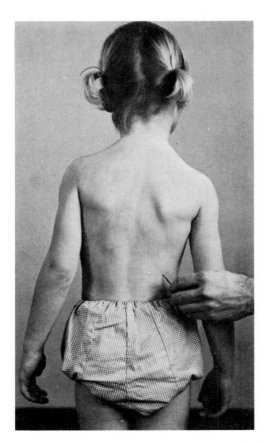

Above, left to right:

Fig. 41. Elicitation of the abdominal skin reflex in the right lower quadrant.

Fig. 42. Elicitation of the cremasteric reflex: position of the testicles before stimulation of the inner side of the upper leg.

Fig. 43. On scratching the inner side of the upper leg, the testicle on the same side is elevated.

Fig. 44 (*left*). Elicitation of the Galant response on the right.

Galant Response (Fig. 44)

Procedure

The examiner takes a pin and scratches slowly along a paravertebral line about 5cm from the midline from shoulder to buttock.

Response

The spine curves in with the concavity on the stimulated side. Only an immediate tonic response in one plane can be considered; other movements may occur as a result of tickling and cannot be interpreted as a Galant response.

Recording

    0 = absent.

    1 = barely discernible incurvation.

    2 = marked incurvation.

Significance

The Galant response is found occasionally in children younger than five, but is usually absent in older children and its presence suggests a delay in neurological maturation. Absence of the abdominal skin reflex may be due to spinal dysfunction at specific levels; a supraspinal lesion may modify the excitability of the spinal centre of the reflex. However, depression or absence may well be due to non-neurological causes (*e.g.* acute surgical problem, distended bladder, surgical scarring of the skin, strong distension of the abdominal muscles caused by ascites). Absence of the cremasteric reflex may be due to non-neurological causes such as cold, nervousness, hydrocele or cryptorchidism.

The abdominal skin reflex and the cremasteric reflex should be symmetrical; asymmetries may be of significance if other lateralised signs in the same pattern occur.

The segmental levels for the abdominal skin reflex are T7-L1, for the Galant response T3-L1 and for the cremasteric reflex L1 and L2.

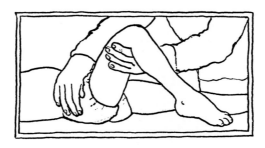

CHAPTER 9

Assessment of the Child Lying

Behavioural State and Social Responsiveness
The optimal state of the child for the following series of tests is 0, though the tests are possible if social responsiveness is 1.

Position
The child must lie prone on the examination table with his head centred.

Age
These tests are suitable for all children aged three to 12, unless otherwise stated.

Examination of the Spine

Procedure
The examiner palpates the spinous processes, paying special attention to the lower lumbar and upper sacral vertebrae. As he does so, the child is asked to move his back sideways, to bend it and to hyperextend it. Particular attention should also be paid to the occurrence of scoliosis, especially if it was present when the child was standing.

Recording
Any abnormalities must be noted and described, including a missing spinous process or any limitation of movement.

Significance
A missing spinous process may indicate a spina bifida occulta and further X-ray analysis is necessary. Similarly, further exploration, *e.g.* X-rays, is necessary if there is any limitation of spinal movement. A scoliosis that persists in the lying position is generally caused by a skeletal abnormality.

Posture of the Legs and Feet

Procedure
The examiner looks for any asymmetries in the posture of the legs and feet, making sure that the child is lying straight with his legs relaxed; this can be confirmed by passively rotating the feet. After examination of the hip joint (see page 86), the child is asked to turn over so that an inspection can be carried out in the supine position. (During the manoeuvre of turning over, the presence or absence of trunk rotation is noted.)

Recording

An asymmetrical posture of legs and feet is described by scoring for abduction, adduction, flexion, extension, exorotation and endorotation respectively; the scores range from 0 to 2, 0 being the neutral position.

Significance

In hemisyndromes, an asymmetrical posture of the legs and feet in the lying position (prone or supine) may be present as the only postural manifestation. However, it must be stressed again that in most instances a single finding is of no clinical significance and must therefore be dealt with very cautiously. Absent or insufficient trunk rotation may be caused by nervous tension, pain, skeletal anomalies, or mild hypertonia (where other neurological signs should be present).

Examination of the Hip Joints (Fig. 45)

Procedure

After inspection of the posture of the legs, the examiner stabilizes the child's pelvis with one hand and retroflexes the upper leg with the other hand. After the child has turned over into the supine position, the examiner flexes and extends the upper leg, and tests for abduction and adduction of the hip joint. By rotating the lower leg (with the knee bent), exo- and endorotation of the upper leg and the hip joint are tested.

Recording

The same criteria are applied as in the assessment of other joints (see 'Resistance against Passive Movements', page 24).

Significance

Asymmetrical findings at the hip joint may suggest a lateralisation, but orthopaedic causes must first be excluded.

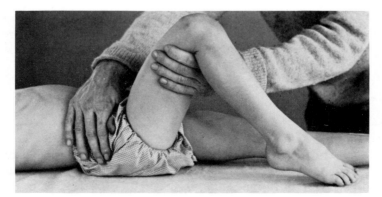

Fig. 45. Examination of resistance to passive movements in the right hip. Flexion, abduction, adduction and rotation are tested with the child in the supine position.

It is essential that the pelvis be kept fixed so that movements of the pelvis do not camouflage limitation of movement by the hip.

Knee-heel Test (Figs. 46 and 47)

Age

This test is suitable for children aged six to 12. In younger children the test described on page 30 (kicking) can be used instead of this test, to gain information about the co-ordination of the legs and feet.

Procedure

The child is asked to lie on his back with his arms by his sides. He is then asked to put the heel of one foot on the knee of the other leg and to keep it there. After a few seconds, he is asked to move his heel down his leg towards the foot without losing contact with the leg. The test is repeated three times for each leg.

Response

All movements should be smooth and steady.

Recording

Accurate placing: $0 =$ accurate placing each time.
                      $1 =$ one or two errors of placement.
                      $2 =$ more than two errors of placement.

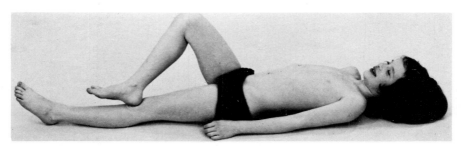

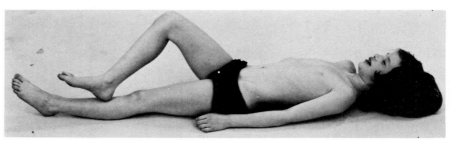

Fig. 46. The child closes her eyes and places one heel on the knee of the other leg.
Fig. 47. She moves her foot down her shin, keeping her eyes closed.

87

Sliding heel down leg: 0 = smooth and steady, no slips.
1 = one or two slips.
2 = more than two slips; unable to keep heel in contact with lower leg.

Significance

This is a useful test of co-ordination of the legs in which cerebellar and proprioceptive functions play a part. Obviously muscular weakness and hypotonia or hypertonia must be excluded. Hip deformities or skeletal anomalies may also hamper an adequate performance. An intention tremor may be observed in severe cases of ataxia, but this condition falls outside the scope of the present book. An asymmetrical performance related to dominance may be expected in six to seven-year-olds. In children over seven, asymmetry reflects an impairment of the co-ordination of one leg. It has to be kept in mind that disturbances of sensory qualities of any source (*e.g.* blisters on the heel) may lead to a bad performance on this test. Deficiencies in the knee-heel test of clinical significance rarely occur as an isolated phenomenon. Usually

Fig. 48. A seven-year-old child can sit up without the help of hands, keeping her legs in contact with the floor.

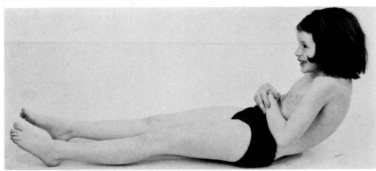

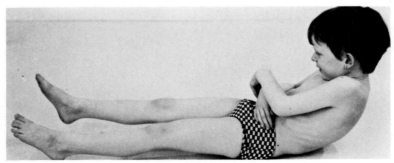

Fig. 49. A five-year-old can only sit up without the help of hands by lifting his legs from the floor.

there will be difficulties in walking, walking on tiptoe and heels, standing on one leg and hopping as well.

Sitting up without the Help of Hands (Figs. 48 and 49)

Procedure

Still lying on his back, the child is asked to sit up without supporting himself with his hands.

Recording

    0 = cannot sit up without support of hands.
    1 = sits up without support of hands, but lifts legs.
    2 = sits up without support of hands, and without lifting legs.

When sitting up without support of the hands is accompanied by lifting of the legs, this must be recorded as symmetrical or asymmetrical and the latter described further.

Significance

Many children under the age of six may not be able to perform this test, and the examiner may assist by putting his hand under the child's head, while the child keeps his hands folded on his abdomen. Lifting of the legs may still be observed. Over the age of seven or eight, most children can sit up without lifting their legs. An asymmetrical lifting of the legs or a symmetrical exaggerated lifting may be due to cerebellar dysfunction.

At the end of this section of the examination, the child may get dressed again.

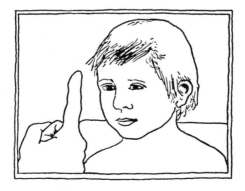

CHAPTER 10

Assessment of the Head

Behavioural State and Social Responsiveness
The optimal state of the child for the following series of tests is 0, though the tests are possible if social responsiveness is 1.

Age
These tests are suitable for all children aged three to 12.

Position
The position of the child is not important. The assessment can be carried out with the child standing beside the sitting examiner. The head should be centred and symmetrical in relation to the body.

Musculature of the Face

Procedure
The examiner must observe the facial musculature at rest and then during voluntary and emotional movements. For this purpose, the child is asked to show his teeth, frown, blow out his cheeks and then close his eyes. After the last instruction, the examiner presses in the child's cheeks and carefully tries to open his eyes. Emotional movements can be observed during laughing and crying.

Recording
Facial musculature is scored three times for asymmetry: at rest, during voluntary movements and during emotional movements.
    0 = no asymmetry.
    1 = slight asymmetry.
    2 = marked asymmetry.

Significance
Unilateral peripheral facial palsies show an asymmetry in both upper and lower parts of the face, whereas a supranuclear lesion shows ipsilateral asymmetry, especially on the lower part of the face. In these cases, the aspect of the facial musculature during emotional movements may be relatively less affected. However, when a nuclear or peripheral lesion is involved the face is affected at all times.
    It is often difficult to assess the symmetry or asymmetry of the neuromuscular functioning of the facial musculature, as many children may have a somewhat asymmetrically shaped skull and face. It may occasionally be necessary to measure the distance between the lateral corner of the eye and the corner of the mouth on each

side of the face, and the distance between the ear and the corner of the mouth. It is always worth inspecting the child's head from above to detect any sign of plagiocephaly which might influence the symmetry of the face. From the age of four years, some children may develop habitual, often asymmetrical, features without any clear neurological significance.

EYES

Position (Fig. 50)

Procedure

The examiner must look for concomitant or non-concomitant strabismus. Slight squints may be detected by looking for symmetry of the corneal reflections. The 'cover test' may be used to detect latent strabismus or heterophoria: each eye is covered in turn while the child looks at a distant object (which does not require convergence). A slight movement may be observed in the uncovered eye either immediately after the other eye is covered, or more often in the covered eye when the cover is removed. The slight movements are often best seen by looking at the corneal reflections. This test is based on the fact that in heterophoria, external eye muscle activity is needed to prevent diplopia, even when the eyes are 'resting'. When one eye is covered, this necessity disappears and the eye muscles can relax. As soon as the cover is removed, contraction of one or more of the eye muscles becomes necessary again, manifesting itself in a slight movement of the eye. The eye which shows movements is the eye with heterophoria. Latent strabismus is apparently a frequently occurring condition,

Fig. 50. Position of the eyes for looking at a distance.

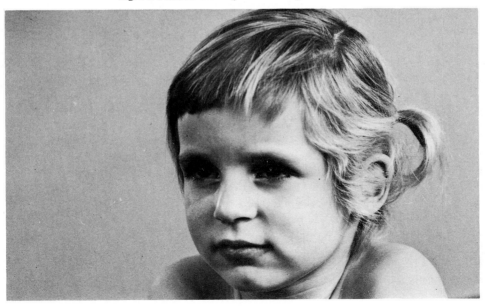

which becomes more evident when the child is tired. Therefore, it is advisable to take into account the time of the day at which the assessment takes place, and the previous activities of the child.

When the eye drifts towards the temporal side, the condition is known as exophoria; to the nasal side it is known as esophoria; upwards as hyperphoria and downwards as hypophoria.

If the eye muscles are not able to bring the visual axes to bear upon the same point, squint or strabismus is present (exotropia, esotropia, hypertropia or hypotropia respectively). In this event, the only way to avoid diplopia is to suppress one image, which leads to a reduction of visual acuity in the squinting eye.

Latent squint may also be observed during the tests for fixation (see below) and convergence (see page 94).

Recording

The presence or absence of heterophoria, concomitant strabismus or non-concomitant strabismus must be recorded. Where present, the eye involved and the type of heterophoria or squint must be described. In the case of non-concomitant strabismus, the eye muscles involved must be described by observing the movements the child is able to make when following an object in his visual field.

Significance

The detection of heterophoria is most important since its presence may hamper the child's ability in close work such as reading, drawing and writing, the muscular strain required leading to fatigue. An accurate estimate of visual acuity (see page 98) is an essential part of assessing how much the eye has deteriorated as a result of a manifest strabismus; in such a case, there is usually an impairment of visual acuity in one eye, especially in children aged five and over. However, amblyopia ex anopsia does not necessarily occur in children aged three or four, since these children often use both eyes alternately (*i.e.* alternate monocular vision).

In true concomitant strabismus, the angle between the two axes should remain constant over the entire range of eye movements, though this need not be exactly so. Concomitant strabismus may be due to optic, sensory, anatomic or nervous causes, but the cause is often unknown, especially in the case of congenital strabismus. A hereditary factor is often present, while it may also be found in children with a history of a birth trauma or short gestation.

In non-concomitant strabismus the angle between the eye-axes changes according to the direction of the gaze. In mild cases the strabismus may disappear in some position of the eyes, but it will then be maximal in the gaze-direction opposite to that position. For example in the case of a (mild) abducens paresis (VIth cranial nerve) of the left eye, the strabismus will be minimal or even absent on looking to the right; it will be present on looking straight forward, and it will be maximal on looking to the left side, *i.e.* to the side of the paretic muscle. Non-concomitant strabismus may result from oculo-paresis due to various causes (*e.g.* congenital or traumatic factors, disease of the orbita, intoxications, infectious diseases, diseases of the central nervous system or eye muscle diseases). Of particular interest is a generally benign and often transient paresis of the VIth cranial nerve some weeks after an otitis media or upper respiratory infection. A paresis of the ocular muscles of long standing may eventually result in a concomitant strabismus (Fig. 51).

Fixation

Procedure

The child is asked to fixate an object (such as the point of a pencil) which is held in front of his eyes for 15 seconds at a distance of about 40cm. Three aspects are considered: deviation of one or both eyes; choreiform movements (*i.e.* jerky movements of both eyes which occur irregularly and arhythmically); and manifest strabismus.

Recording

Deviation, choreiform movements and squint are recorded as absent or present, and the involved eye and direction of the deviation or squint are specified.

Significance

Deviation of one eye during fixation may be due to a latent strabismus (heterophoria) or to an ocular paresis (see above). The significance of choreiform movements is discussed on page 100 and strabismus on page 92.

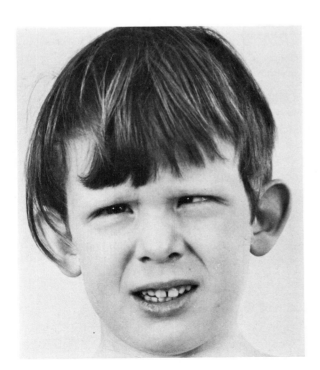

Fig. 51. Position of the eyes in a boy with a longstanding paresis of the VIth cranial nerve on the left side. The strabismus is concomitant.

Visual Pursuit Movements

Procedure

The examiner moves a small object in front of the child in both the horizontal and the vertical plane. The child is asked to follow the object with his eyes, keeping his head still. Two aspects are assessed: the quality and the range of the ocular movements. Movements may be smooth, ataxic or choreiform. The last category is used for vertical jerky movements when the eyes move sideways and horizontal jerky movements when the eyes move upwards and downwards, occurring in both eyes simultaneously.

Recording

Abnormal following is described and any restriction of the full range of movements is recorded. Choreiform and ataxic eye movements are recorded as absent or present. During this test the examiner can also ascertain the presence of concomitant or non-concomitant strabismus, and in the latter case, which muscles are involved (see Table V). In children with latent strabismus (but apparently also independent of that condition) a type of 'imbalance' of the eyes may be present. During following a moving object the eye-axes of both eyes remain parallel over the whole range of movements, but this parallelism is lost at the end and beginning of the movement. This occurs especially during the return movement after looking sideways. One eye seems to change its movement pattern faster than the other eye, which may even give the impression of remaining static, while the first eye moves. Usually the contralateral eye (*i.e.* the eye in the nasal position) remains static or moves less. 'Imbalance' is recorded as absent or present.

Significance

Deviations in the visual pursuit of an object may be due to paresis of the ocular muscles. Diplopia is rarely found in children because of rapid cortical suppression of one image. Ataxic movements may be due to impaired co-ordination of the eye muscles. The significance of choreiform movements is discussed on page 110.

'Imbalance' can be a sign of a latent strabismus, but seems to exist without heterophoria. Its presence is often associated with other signs of minor neurological dysfunction. However, its significance for reading difficulties is not well understood.

Convergence (Fig. 52)

Procedure

An object is held at a distance of about 50cm from the child and is moved towards him.

Response

The eyes converge on the object and the pupils contract.

Recording

0 = no convergence visible at all.

94

TABLE V

Action of individual eye muscles

M. rectus lateralis:	to the temporal side
M. rectus medialis:	to the nasal side
M. rectus superior:	upwards and slightly inwards
M. rectus inferior:	downwards and slightly inwards
M. obliques superior:	downwards and slightly outwards
M. obliques inferior:	upwards and slightly outwards

1 = unable to maintain convergence with the object closer than 15cm to the eyes.

2 = maintains convergence of both eyes on an object to about 10cm in front of the eyes.

Any differences in convergence between the eyes are recorded. Pupillary reaction is also recorded as absent or present.

Significance

Movements should be the same on both sides. A symmetrical weakness is

Fig. 52. Convergence of the eyes in looking at a close object. Compare with Fig. 51.

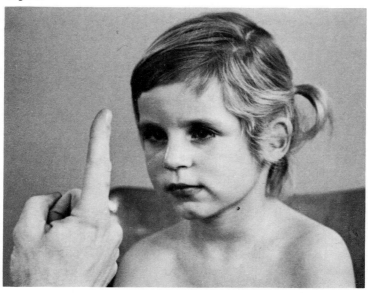

generally of central origin; an asymmetrical weakness may be due to a paresis of an ocular muscle or to amblyopia of one eye. Weakness of convergence may also be caused by myopia or severe hypermetropia.

In cases of exophoria, convergence demands more muscle activity than usual and may therefore be rather weak; conversely, in cases of esophoria, convergence may be very strong.

The clinical significance of weakness or absence of convergence is not clear. It is said that the absence or weakness of convergence may be due to midbrain lesions (Paine and Oppé 1966), for instance as a post-encephalitic symptom. Theoretically it is possible that such weakness of convergence may give rise to difficulties as far as close work is concerned, due to fatigue of the eye muscles. It is also possible that suppression of one eye-image would occur, which may even lead to amblyopia. There is, however, no convincing evidence for either possibility. Especially among pre-school children and young school children (ages five and six) convergence weakness may occasionally be found as an isolated finding and without any complaint or objective difficulty whatever.

Contraction of the pupils (miosis) during convergence is a sign of the accommodation of the lens, which is linked with the activity of the ciliary body. Absence of miosis may be due to the use of drugs, to a functional disturbance of the intraocular muscles, or to a mechanical cause.

Nystagmus

Nystagmus consists of involuntary oscillatory eye movements, usually with a slow and a rapid component. The latter is used to give the direction of the nystagmus.

Procedure

The examiner holds an object about 50cm from the child and notes the occurrence of spontaneous nystagmus. The child is then asked to keep his head still while the examiner moves the object 45° sideways and to fixate on the object for about ten seconds in the new position. This is repeated at a 45° angle on the other side. A nystagmus occurring in these latter situations is called a directional nystagmus.

Recording

The presence or absence of spontaneous and directional nystagmus is recorded and the direction of the rapid component described if present. The intensity of the nystagmus should also be described and a note made of any asymmetries.

Significance

A horizontal, pendular nystagmus which is present from shortly after birth is called 'congenital nystagmus'. Its aetiology is obscure; the intensity may be affected by the position of the head. Nearly always, vision is impaired. Spontaneous non-congenital nystagmus may be due to disturbances of the vestibular system, which may be of infectious, toxic, traumatic or other origin.

In most cases, directional nystagmus is of vestibular origin but it may be due to a functional weakness of the eye muscles.

Optokinetic Nystagmus

Procedure

It is of little practical value, within the scope of this book, to introduce complicated techniques for the accurate evaluation of optokinetic nystagmus. However, it may be useful to know whether this nystagmus can be elicited laterally and vertically with the same frequency and intensity. For this purpose, it suffices to move a picture strip in front of the child's eyes in all four directions at a distance of about 40cm. Provided that the speed of movement of the strip is approximately the same in all directions, the optokinetic nystagmus elicited in this way should show the same frequency.

Recording

The presence or absence of horizontal and vertical optokinetic nystagmus is recorded and any asymmetry is noted. A difference in frequency between the eyes should also be recorded.

Significance

Horizontal optokinetic nystagmus should be elicitable in this way. Vertical optokinetic nystagmus is often more difficult to observe, especially when moving the strip downwards. A different frequency between the two eyes is always pathological and should arouse the suspicion of an intracerebral lesion. Asymmetry of the optokinetic nystagmus in opposite directions may be of cerebral or peripheral origin, *e.g.* functional disturbances in the optical and/or vestibular systems.

A faulty response on this test may also be the consequence of diminished vision in one or both eyes.

Pupillary Reactions

Procedure

The size of the pupil is recorded and then a bright light is flashed into one eye only and the reactions of both pupils observed. This is repeated with the other eye. The child should be in such a position that light from outside or from a ceiling-light falls on both eyes equally.

Response

Pupillary reactions may be absent, slow or fast. If a light is thrown into one eye (direct reaction), the contralateral pupil (indirect reaction) should contract simultaneously with the stimulated pupil.

Recording

The size of the pupil is recorded as small, medium or large, and irregularities are described.

Direct pupillary reaction to light: 0 = absent.
    1 = weak.
    2 = strong.

Indirect pupillary reaction to light: 0 = absent.

                                                  1 = weak.

                                                  2 = strong.

Significance

Reaction to light should be prompt and marked. No contraction of the pupils may be due to peripheral or central causes. A negative indirect reaction results from unilateral blindness, caused by a lesion of the optic nerve. A weak and slow contraction may be due to drugs, infections, post-infectious conditions or a generalized depression of nervous functions.

Visual Acuity

Procedure

The examiner can test the older child's visual acuity by use of the Snellen Letter Charts. The Stycar tests can be used for children who cannot read letters (Sheridan 1969). This test, in which the child matches letters, makes it relatively easy to test visual acuity down to the age of three. These methods often give better results than the well known illiterate E-chart or picture chart.

Recording

Visual acuity is recorded as normal or abnormal, in which case a description is required.

Significance

The optimal 6/6 vision should not be expected before the age of six or seven; children younger than this are often hypermetropic. However, in cases of doubt, referral to an ophthalmologist for skiascopy is necessary (see page 9).

Visual Field (Figs. 53 and 54)

Procedure

The examiner sits down with the child standing in front of him so that their faces are on the same level. He asks the child to fixate on his nose (or a small object held about 40cm in front of the child). Then he moves a small object from one side of and from behind the child's head so that it gradually enters his visual field. The child is instructed to grasp the object as soon as he catches sight of it. The test is carried out from each side and from above the child's head. By sitting immediately in front of the child, the examiner is able to observe whether the child fixates well. A crude impression can thus be obtained about the child's visual fields. The test can be repeated with objects of different sizes and colours. Children aged over six may be asked to cover one eye with their hands or a wooden spoon.

Response

The normal angle of vision to the side is between 60° and 80° and above is about 45°. It is often unnecessary to wait for actual grasping. Usually an orienting response

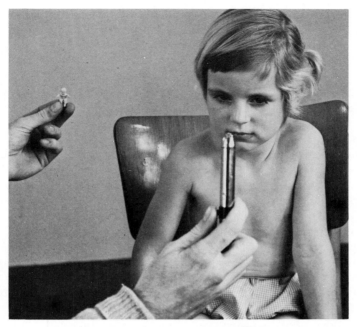

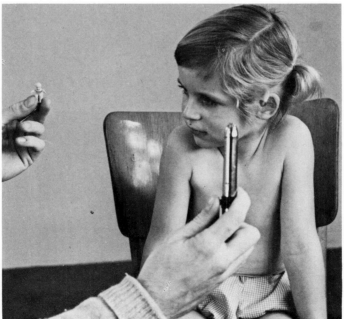

Fig. 53 (*above*). Position for the evaluation of the visual fields: the child looks at an object held in front of her while a toy is brought nearer from behind.

Fig. 54 (*below*). The response.

occurs as soon as the object enters the visual field, and that causes a movement of the eye towards the stimulus. Presence of this orienting is sufficient for a positive score on this test.

Recording
The estimated angle at which the child perceives the object is recorded after each test and noted to be normal or abnormal.

Significance
The most common visual field defects in children are homonymous hemianopia, which generally accompanies spastic hemiplegia, and bitemporal hemianopia resulting from tumours near the optic chiasm, which may arise quite insidiously. Lesser defects, such as quadrantic defects of the visual fields, are rare (deriving from craniopharyngioma or a temporal lobe tumour involving the optic radiation). Although such cases evidently surpass the bounds of minor dysfunction, a visual field defect may be the first clinical sign. The above test is sufficient for routine purposes, but if there is any doubt, perimetry should be carried out; however, this may be rather difficult and unreliable in children below the age of six or seven.

The examiner must bear in mind that diminished visual acuity may be responsible for diminished visual fields.

As with other tests of visuo-ocular abilities, any abnormal findings warrant referral to an ophthalmologist.

Choreiform Movements of the Face

Procedure
Throughout the examination of the eyes, the presence or absence of choreiform movements of the face should be assessed. There may be some difficulty in differentiating between choreiform movements and 'tics', especially in the upper part of the face, but the latter tend to show a more stereotyped pattern.

Recording
Choreiform movements are recorded as absent or present.

Significance
See pages 54 and 110.

Funduscopy
Funduscopy is carried out as the final assessment of the entire examination (see page 107), but may usefully be discussed here. It is not usually necessary to dilate the pupils pharmacologically for a routine inspection of the optic disc; however, in cases of doubt it may be necessary to use a mydriatic agent.

A discussion of all the different types of anomalies of the retina is beyond the scope of this book. For a routine screening it is sufficient to examine the fundus for papilloedema, which may indicate increased intracranial pressure and in rare cases may be the first manifestation of an extensive intracranial lesion. When other anomalies of the retina are present, such as black spots, white streaks, vascular anomalies, often a more specific examination must be carried out. It must be borne in mind that anomalies in refraction may considerably hamper inspection of the fundus.

EARS

Auditory Acuity

Procedure

The examiner sits about six yards away from the child and in a low voice pronounces test words of different sound spectra ('66', '100', '99') including single consonantal sounds ('sss', 'rrr', 'mmm') and vowel sounds ('uuuu', 'aaaa'). Each ear is tested in turn, the child keeping the other ear covered with his hand and repeating the sounds as heard. Children below the age of six may be asked to point to pictures; schemes suited to the English language have been devised by Sheridan (1969).

Recording

Auditory acuity in each ear is recorded as correct, dubious or failed.
   0 = correct.
   1 = dubious.
   2 = failed.

Significance

A dubious response indicates the need for further audiological examination. It is of course highly desirable for pure tone audiometry to be carried out as a routine part of the examination, but the doctor should always screen hearing himself.

Localisation of Sound

Procedure

The examiner stands behind the child and gently rings a small bell on each side of his head and then above his head.

Response

The child is asked to point towards the place where the sound comes from. He is not expected to say 'left', 'right' or 'above', since this is not a test of his ability to comprehend and distinguish these concepts.

Recording
   0 = no localisation at all.
   1 = localisation correct laterally.
   2 = localisation correct in all directions.

Significance

Most but not all children aged five and over are able to achieve accurate vertical localisation; this may be regarded as a maturational phenomenon. However, a

101

negative response is of dubious significance in our present state of knowledge. Failure to locate sounds in any lateral position indicates the need for further audiological analysis.

MOUTH

Tongue

Procedure

The child is asked to stick out his tongue and keep it as still as possible. After about ten seconds, voluntary movements of discomfort may occur. Any occurrence of involuntary movements should be carefully noted, and then the child is asked to move his tongue from side to side, touching the corners of his mouth. Subsequently he is asked to move his tongue along his teeth in the upper and lower jaws in a near circular movement. Finally, he is asked to protrude it as far as possible.

Recording

Choreiform movements:	absent or present.
Fasciculations:	absent or present.
Smoothness of movements:	absent or present.

Significance

A discussion of the significance of choreiform and athetoid movements can be found on pages 53 and 110.

Fasciculations are asynchronous, irregular, rapid twitches of very small parts of the tongue. The tongue is the only muscle in which they can be observed, myograms being necessary for other muscles. They must be differentiated from choreiform movements which occur in more extended areas of the tongue and lead to gross movements. Their significance is also different, since fasciculations are generally a sign of a serious, progressive disease (*e.g.* bulbar disorders).

Children over the age of seven or eight should be able to move their tongue smoothly from side to side and to protrude it for more than one third of its visible length. Awkwardness of tongue movements, and also drooling, which is often a sign of disturbances of swallowing, may be related to speech difficulties. A short frenulum of the tongue is in the majority of cases of little clinical significance.

Pharyngeal Arches

Procedure

The child is asked to open his mouth as wide as possible so that the examiner can inspect the pharyngeal arches at rest. Then the child is asked to say 'aaaa' so that the examiner may inspect them during movement.

Recording

The arches are recorded as symmetrical or asymmetrical and described in the latter instance.

Significance

Asymmetries of the pharyngeal arches, particularly during phonation, may be related to difficulties in speech and speech development. However, for several weeks or even months after tonsillectomy, some children may show temporary asymmetry of the movement of the arches, without evident impairment of speech or swallowing.

SPONTANEOUS MOTOR ACTIVITY

At this juncture, it is important for a reassessment of spontaneous motor activity to be made. Children with minor nervous dysfunction sometimes show a particularly marked increase or even a decrease in this field.

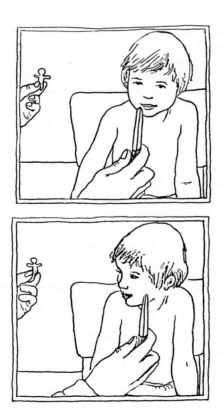

CHAPTER 11

General Data

When the assessment of the head has been concluded (except for funduscopy), the neurological examination is virtually completed. However, there are certain aspects of the general paediatric and developmental examination which may yield important information to the neurologist. For instance, the relationship of the child's weight to his height is relevant to an assessment of the quality of motility, since it is obvious that an overweight child may show a different quality of motility than a child of slender build. For example, a fat child will often show a lower speed of movement, while a slender child may be more agile. In the case of clumsiness this difference may result in different phenotypical behaviour, for instance show coarse and awkward movement patterns versus very fast, abrupt and 'hurry-scurry' motor behaviour. It is useful, therefore, to weigh and measure the child, and also to measure the circumference of the skull (for micro- or macrocephaly) and to describe any abnormalities in the shape of the skull (for plagiocephaly, synostosis of a single suture, etc.). In clinical practice, abnormal findings as a result of the general paediatric examination with regard to the lungs and heart, the mucous membranes, ears and throat and general malformations may be significant and can usefully be recorded.

In practice, too, the examiner may wish to employ some of the tests of the type described in the Introduction (Chapter 1), which are not satisfactory in strict neurological terms, but which may yield valuable information if carefully interpreted. Such tests are often behavioural items which are also the appropriate sphere of the psychologist. Each examiner will develop his own preferences in this sort of testing, and objective data are lacking for guidance. The following may provide a useful outline.

Dominance

In a discussion of this problem, a careful distinction must be made between 'dominance', which we use to imply something about neurological organisation, suggesting that one hemisphere is superior to the other in controlling particular motor functions, and 'preference' which describes the hand, foot or eye the child prefers to use for particular tasks.

Hand Preference

We use three tests of hand preference: drawing (which also serves for an assessment of fine motor co-ordination), writing, and cutting a piece of paper. The necessary implements are handed to the child in a neutral position, with no bias to right or left. Children over the age of five or six can also be asked to catch a ball (approximately ten times in each hand), so that the most capable hand may be recorded.

Foot Preference

Foot preference is more difficult to assess. A child may prefer one leg for kicking and the other for standing on one leg, while older children are able to use both legs alternately for kicking (and both hands for catching a ball) without demonstrating any particular preference. We have found that of a mixed sample of 150 five-year-olds, 28 per cent hopped more than 13 times on their left leg, and 39.5 per cent hopped more than 13 times on their right leg. Often, an accurate assessment of preference can be obtained by asking the child which is his 'best' leg. The development of laterality of the legs appears to be different for balance and for voluntary motor movements. Children below the age of seven years often use their preferred leg for maintaining balance, and therefore tend to use their non-preferred leg for kicking a football. Over seven years of age balance is usually well established and children usually use their preferred leg for voluntary motor movements, such as kicking a football, or hopping. So it may be found that a child of about seven prefers one leg (usually his leg of preference) for standing on, and the other for kicking a football. Older children may start to stand on their non-preferred leg, but they start to hop on the preferred leg. It can therefore be difficult to assess the leg of preference accurately, especially at ages under seven, and in motor-retarded older children.

Eye Preference

To assess eye preference, we ask the child to look with one eye through a short tube or a hole in a piece of paper, first with the examiner holding the tube and then holding it himself. Some children may be able to use either eye at will. It is possible that hand preference in holding the tube may influence the choice of eye for looking. Clearly, refraction anomalies and other possible sources of difference in the visual capacities of the eyes must be excluded prior to the assessment.

Significance

Where preference is consistent, it would seem reasonable to talk of dominance. The age at which dominance is established is a matter for debate, as is the question of mixed laterality, but it appears that preferences as regards certain actions may be well established by the age of three or four. 'Handedness' is established at about age six and 'footedness' at age eight. Despite our lack of knowledge about the nature of dominance, it is important to record it, and to attempt to distinguish it from asymmetry due to neurological damage.

It is often stated that left-handedness, or crossed eye- and hand-laterality or hand-foot laterality occur more often in so-called minor brain damaged children (see *e.g.* Paine and Oppé 1966), which may sometimes even lead to the interpretation of left-handedness or crossed laterality as a possible sign of minor neurological dysfunction. However, this is really an inversion of the argument. There is no reason to surmise that findings of left-handedness or crossed laterality are indicative of minor neurological dysfunction. This is convincingly demonstrated by Rutter *et al.* (1970). As the majority of humans are 'right-handed', although the estimation of handedness depends largely on the battery of tests used for the assessment (see Touwen 1972, 1979), it stands to reason that a shift to left-handedness as a result of slight damage to the left brain will occur more often than the other way round. However, this is not to say that any left-handedness can be accounted for by brain damage. In our experience left-handedness or crossed laterality as a single finding has no clinical significance, and cannot be regarded as a sign of minor neurological dysfunction. When other signs of minor neurological dysfunction are present, left-handedness or crossed laterality may be interpreted as an associated minor sign of neurological dysfunction only if it fits into the pattern of signs formed by the other findings, and in the absence of a family history of left-handedness. In cases of mixed handedness (ambidexterity) one has to be alert to the possibility of training effects for the use of the right hand. Pure or absolute left-handedness or right-handedness, meaning that the other hand is of no practical use at all, is virtually always based on a neurological dysfunction.

In children below six it has to be borne in mind that on the side of the preferred hand or/and leg, muscle tone and reflex intensity may be slightly different (generally somewhat higher) than on the side of the non-preferred arm or/and leg. This may even simulate the presence of a slight hemisyndrome.

Fine Motor Co-ordination

It must be borne in mind that any impressions formed about the child's agility in tasks such as dressing, handling buttons or tying shoe-laces must not be considered as solid data measuring well-known neurological phenomena. Such activities are highly complex and depend on many often inextricably interwoven factors. A recording of the child's manipulative abilities may be of some interest, however, and may also be observed during the assessment of hand preference for example. Small objects should be picked up in a 'pincer grasp' (*i.e.* opposition of the tips of the thumb and the index finger); long and narrow objects like a pencil, however, are often picked up with the thumb in opposition to three or four fingers. Children of five years and more should be able to hold the pencil between the thumb and index finger, whereas younger children often hold it between the second and third finger, and very young or severely retarded children may use the whole hand for drawing. However, observation of drawing does not generally add any clear information about neurological functions which cannot be obtained by more standardised neurological means.

Sensory Examination

As stressed in Chapter 3 (p. 8), specific use of classical neurological tests such as two-point discrimination, tactile sensation with cotton wool, or pain and temperature perception have not proved particularly useful in the neurological evaluation of children suspected of minor neurological dysfunction, as, particularly in the age-group for which the present manual is intended, the results are often unreliable. Nevertheless, during the routine examination it is possible to make some general observations about the child's sensory functions. At some point in the examination the examiner can touch the child with a cold metal object and note his reaction and comments, if any. He can also record whether the child is sensitive to light touch and to the pin used in testing for the abdominal skin, Galant and cremasteric reflexes. Where there is any cause for doubt as to a child's sensitivity to tactile sensations, pain

106

or differences in temperature, a more extensive examination should be carried out, but, as yet, no reliable methods of examination have been devised, particularly for children with learning and/or behavioural difficulties.

In older children, kinesthesia and sense of position in the thumbs and big toes can be tested by gently moving a thumb or toe and asking the child if he is aware of the movement. The child should keep his eyes closed during the test. He can then be asked to describe the position in which the examiner is holding the thumb or toe.

It should be borne in mind that the evaluation of sensory functions is difficult and time-consuming, and a special examination-session is needed if one wants to obtain reliable data. During the routine neurological examination the need for a specific assessment of sensory functions can be decided on, and in that case a separate session should be devoted to it, instead of an immediate attempt to obtain some crude information during the routine assessment.

Speech and Language

As mentioned in the Introduction, there may be a close association between neurological dysfunction and speech disorders. Data obtained from an assessment of speech will clearly be relevant to the final assessment of the child with neurological dysfunction. It is usually possible to elicit sufficient speech from the child during the course of the 30 to 40 minute routine examination to decide whether a further intensive speech examination should form part of the assessment of each particular child. The examiner may observe many infantile speech faults such as substitutions, inversion, or perseverations during the neurological assessment, and he should hear enough speech to suspect that the child has difficulties with articulation or to decide that the child's use of language is appropriate to his age. It is a good idea to have toys and pictures in the examination room and to ask the child to name them.

If a child does not talk enough for an assessment to be made, the examiner should consult with psychological colleagues carrying out a behavioural assessment of the child. This is particularly important if the child has not spoken well. If the psychologist has also noted difficulties, speech and language specialists should commonly be called in to consultation. If there is any suspicion of dysarthria, a close examination of the mouth, tongue and palate is clearly important, and additional tests, probably with the aid of an ear, nose and throat specialist and a speech therapist may have to be carried out.

All these functions are recorded as indicated on the proforma (see page 133), and funduscopy can then be carried out as described in Chapter 10.

CHAPTER 12

Interpretation and Diagnosis

Introduction

Obviously, a neurological examination must be followed by an interpretation of the findings. One should remember that our main purpose has been to design a descriptive examination. In the case of minor neurological deviations it is wrong to make a hurried interpretation, as an interpretation arrived at during, and not after, an assessment is a dangerous thing. This is particularly true of patients with no complaints of a recognisable neurological origin, *i.e.* the majority of children with behavioural and learning difficulties. Often the significance of the findings can only be evaluated after the comprehensive and descriptive examination is completed, when the examiner tries to see if the neurological data can be fitted into a meaningful pattern. A traditional diagnosis, however, is not always feasible. In this case we group together special signs and symptoms in an attempt to identify specific entities which we refer to as 'syndromes', and which may be significant in the dynamics of the child's problems.

Before discussion of this procedure, some remarks must be made about the additional information one gathers to supplement the findings of the neurological examination; this must be considered together with the interpretation of findings for the final diagnosis. It is obvious that the child's full history is of prime importance and it should be obtained from the child's parents, preferably at the end of the examination in order to avoid bias. This is particularly important if one is looking for minor deviations of optimal functioning in children with behavioural difficulties but without specific neurological complaints. However, it must be stressed that the relationship between a neurological disorder in the history (measles encephalitis, for instance) and the set of behavioural problems for which a child is referred, is often unclear. The neurological disorder may have resulted in structural changes in the nervous system, which will undoubtedly have influenced the subsequent 'history of the brain'. However, it may also have caused environmental changes during the child's development (stays in hospital, the parents' concern and so on) which can have influenced the child's behavioural development. When signs of neurological dysfunction may be considered as sequelae of the historical event, there may or may not be a relationship between the behavioural problems and the neurological dysfunction (this relationship must be explored further), but a direct causal relationship cannot be surmised without further evidence.

When a young child has been referred to a clinic because of learning and/or behavioural difficulties, various specialist assessments should be made (paediatric, psychological, audiological, ophthalmological, speech and so on); all these must be taken into account when drawing up a final diagnosis. It is very important that some conclusion be made about the child's functioning on the basis of each particular assessment alone. Each assessment must be evaluated before the results are combined and the various examinations should therefore be carried out independently of each other.

Neurological Signs

This book is particularly concerned with the conclusions that may be drawn from neurological signs. As we have emphasised throughout the book, a single non-optimal sign, such as an isolated dorsiflexion of the big toe, or an isolated, exaggerated knee-jerk reflex, rarely has any clinical significance. However, when non-optimal signs are found in combinations, a valuable clinical interpretation may be feasible. Our aim, therefore, is to collect all non-optimal signs, arrange them into syndromes if possible, and then attempt to relate them to other diagnostic information, in order to evaluate them in the child's present set of complaints.

We shall now discuss the various entities which may be distinguished from the ways in which isolated neurological signs tend to cluster. The various groups often show a considerable overlap, although a number of distinct signs of neurological dysfunction may be found which do not seem to be connected at all.

Hemisyndrome

By the terms 'hemisyndrome' or 'lateralisation syndrome', we mean a combination of neurological signs that together form a specific unilateral pattern. It should not be inferred that major functional difficulties are also present; by definition, all hemiplegias fall into the group of hemisyndromes, but a child with a hemisyndrome need not be hemiparetic. For instance, a hemisyndrome may consist of a combination of slightly increased (or decreased) tendon reflexes, slightly increased resistance to passive movements, a dorsiflexion of the big toe and some pronation of one of the extended arms, all on the same side of the body; from a superficial observation of the freemoving child, however, these may be quite inconspicuous. On the other hand, a hemisyndrome may consist of a paretic arm and leg of central origin, or of a unilateral peripheral nerve lesion.

Clearly, the signs which indicate a hemisyndrome may range from the very severe to the very mild. The mild forms do not generally interfere with ordinary everyday activities; fine motor co-ordination may be slightly impaired, but this is not necessarily the case.

The topographical and functional correlation of the different signs will facilitate a differentiation between their central or peripheral origin. As in the case of severe manifestations of hemisyndromes, mild forms may originate from pre- or perinatal brain damage, or may be acquired in infancy or childhood (due to trauma, infections, etc.). It must be borne in mind that mild signs of a hemisyndrome may be the first clinical manifestation of a progressive disorder such as a cerebral tumour, metabolic disorders or leucodystrophies.

Dyskinesia

Dyskinesia may occur in various forms, such as choreo-athetosis, chorea, athetoid cerebral palsy and dystonias, as well as choreiform movements, athetotiform movements, tremor and tics.

In choreo-athetosis, the lesion is situated in the striatum and basal ganglia, often due to kernicterus or perinatal asphyxia. It may be manifest in very severe or very mild form. Children with blood-group incompatibilities who underwent transfusions to prevent kernicterus may well show only very minor signs.

Huntington's chorea and other rare hereditary forms of chorea initially present with minor signs of dyskinesia. Chorea minor (Sydenham's chorea), which is caused by streptococcal infection, may manifest itself in a very mild form, or may present with only mild choreatic movements as a sequela of the acute form.

Athetotiform and choreiform dyskinesias also range from very mild to severe. As mentioned previously (page 53), these terms are derived from the initial likeness to mild forms of athetosis and chorea. The movements are probably due to an instability of motor units. This instability may take the form of a lowered membrane potential of the motor cell itself, or may be related to changes in the excitatory and/or inhibitory input to the motor cell from other nerve cells. These neurophysiological changes may occur without a topographically circumscribed lesion of the brain.

Thus, choreiform movements may be considered as a noise phenomenon in a complex central system, the effect on motor functioning depending on the signal-noise ratio during a given performance. In very delicate motor activity, any non-relevant activity will interfere considerably, while in gross motor activity, the effect will be relatively less because of the higher rate of redundancy; this, at least, is the hypothesis which might explain such clearly demonstrable phenomena. A significant relationship has been found between the hyperexcitability syndrome in the neonatal period and the occurrence of choreiform movements in later life (Prechtl 1965). The aetiology of choreiform movements has not yet been fully explained, but it is evident that pre- and perinatal complications, as well as complications occurring in the first years of life such as severe respiratory diseases, gastrointestinal disturbances or head traumas play some part. A genetic factor may also be involved. It has been shown that the incidence of choreiform movements is two to three times higher in boys (Stemmer 1964).

Athetotiform movements are fairly frequent in children below the age of five to six years. Preliminary data suggest that they occur more frequently among special school pupils than among children attending ordinary primary schools, and that they are closely related to the presence of choreiform movements. The aetiology of athetotiform movements is still obscure. The fact that some children show this type of movement while others do not, and that the movements decrease in intensity and frequency with age, suggest that they are a worthy topic of consideration in relation to minor neurological dysfunction.

A mild degree of resting tremor is often present in school children and characteristically does not interfere with even very fine manipulations, except in some rare instances. However, marked tremor does interfere considerably with fine motor activities. Tremor may occur in any muscle of the body, but it is usually most marked in the arms and fingers.

Associated Movements

Associated movements (known variously as synkinetic movements, co-movements and mirror movements) often accompany voluntary or involuntary movements in young children, generally in contralateral and symmetrical parts of the body. They decrease with age, and their disappearance is reckoned to be a sign of the functional maturation of the nervous system. Several authors have emphasised the possibility of using the occurrence of associated movements over a certain age (which must be specified for each type of movement separately) as a sign of impaired neurological functioning, *i.e.* retardation of the nervous development (Abercrombie *et al.* 1964, Connolly and Stratton 1968, Fog and Fog 1963, Zazzo 1960). These authors have devised special tests for associated movements, but in our experience these tests are time-consuming and we prefer to assess associated movements at the same time as we test other aspects of the nervous system, *e.g.* diadochokinesis, walking on tiptoe and walking on heels.

The mouth-opening finger-spreading test does specifically test for associated movements, but the results should not be taken as a sound indication of the occurrence of associated movements in general, nor should the scoring be immediately related to the results of the tests advocated by other authors. As far as is known at present, there is no direct relationship between the score on the mouth-opening finger-spreading test and the amount of associated movements occuring with diadochokinesis, walking on tiptoe or walking on heels. Our own observations suggest that there is not even any direct relationship between the amount of associated movements in the contralateral arm during the test for diadochokinesis and the amount of associated movements during clenching the fist, and this must be borne in mind when attempting to evaluate the occurrence of associated movements. Many factors may influence the amount of associated movements shown, *e.g.* the complexity of the movement involved, the intensity with which the 'trigger' movement is carried out, the order in which the tasks are presented and the familiarity with the requested 'trigger' movement. Many adults who do not show any associated movements when carrying out the test for diadochokinesis with the preferred hand do show them when carrying out the test with the non-preferred hand, especially if they do the test forcefully. Associated movements may also be seen in the tongue during writing. It does not need to be emphasised that the persistence of marked associated movements may interfere with many other acts.

Associated movements are often more marked on one side of the body and are probably related to cerebral dominance, the movements spreading to one side of the body more easily than to the other. It is not always easy to predict which side will be more affected. In older children, whose cerebral dominance is definitely established, spreading will generally occur from the non-dominant towards the dominant side, and this may be the normal or optimal situation. However, this is not true of all children. Two factors may be involved in these cases: one is the wide variability in the age at which cerebral dominance is established, and the other is the fact that, in many individuals, dominance may not be strictly unilateral. Crossed laterality may occur not only between hands and feet, but in other forms of mixed laterality which are very difficult to demonstrate. Furthermore, the order in which the tests are

111

applied and the skill on the side which has to perform the trigger movements may be of considerable importance in a comparison of associated movements on the left and right side of the body.

It is also possible that a strong asymmetry of associated movements may be part of a hemisyndrome, the neurologically impaired side showing more such movements. A high amount of associated movements may be found in combination with other signs of non-optimal nervous functioning, *e.g.* dyskinesias, co-ordination difficulties and evidence of hemisyndromes, etc. They may also be found in combination with other signs of motor retardation, such as an inability to continue hopping or standing on one leg for a sufficient amount of time or inadequate diadochokinesia, but without specific sign of nervous impairment. In the first instance, there may or may not be some developmental retardation, but clearly signs of nervous dysfunction play a dominant rôle; in the second instance, the developmental lag is the main or even the only feature of the child's neurological functioning. This differentiation is very important, since in the case of nervous dysfunction, the possibility of specific disorders, even progressive ones, must be considered, while developmental retardation may require a very different therapeutic approach.

Developmental Retardation

This term is generally used to include specific signs of mental retardation together with failure to develop certain behavioural skills such as building a tower with ten bricks, drawing a circle inside a square and speaking sentences of a given length at various specific ages. These problems may or may not be associated with neurological retardation. In the context of this book, developmental retardation means only a maturational lag in neurological functions such as walking, hopping, standing on one leg, diadochokinesia or the persistence of infantile reflexes, etc. The importance of the rôle of cerebral dominance in these instances has already been pointed out. Other signs of nervous dysfunction such as dyskinesia, a hemisyndrome or co-ordination difficulties may or may not be present. The possible combination of neurological retardation with mental retardation goes beyond the scope of this book, but it should be borne in mind that the two are not necessarily related.

The importance of an accurate differentiation between signs of neurological retardation that are accompanied by other signs of nervous dysfunction and those that are not has already been stressed (see above). However, developmental retardation may originate in nervous dysfunction due to cerebral damage while few other signs of this dysfunction are evident.

Difficulties in Co-ordination

Here again, it is essential to distinguish between impaired co-ordination and a retardation of co-ordination capabilities. This distinction may be very difficult or even impossible; the existence of other signs of neurological developmental retardation or, alternatively, signs of neurological dysfunction which are not due to developmental retardation may be helpful.

Several aspects of co-ordination may be distinguished, *e.g.* the maintenance of balance, the ability to anticipate shifts in the centre of gravity before making voluntary movements, the co-ordination of rapid rhythmical movements and of fine manipulations, and complex skilled motor performances. The brain structures involved are the proprioceptive system, including the vestibula, the reticular formation and the cerebellum, and, in the case of complex motor behaviour, the parietal lobes.

The major complaint accompanying cases of mild disabilities of motor co-ordination is clumsiness or awkwardness. Fine motor co-ordination and gross motor co-ordination are not necessarily impaired simultaneously and to the same degree. The maturation of normal co-ordination is slow and much training and learning is involved. Walking without support, for instance, usually develops several months after the child can walk holding his mother's hands. A steady gait develops later still, after the acquisition of skilled balance. Fine manipulations such as doing up and undoing buttons should be possible at the age of four, and tying up shoe-laces at the age of six. Diadochokinesia should be smooth and rapid by the age of eight.

It is very useful to make a distinction between co-ordination, in the sense of a well-established balance between agonists and antagonists (*e.g.* in diadochokinesis, which involves the pronator and supinator muscles of the lower arm, or in the knee-heel test, which involves mainly the flexors, extensors and adductors of the leg) and fine manipulative ability, with its more complex motor skills in which a highly differential set of muscles is involved (finger -opposition and follow-a-finger tests, for example). It can be postulated that for carrying out fine manipulations, besides the integrity of the sensorimotor system, the co-ordination of antagonists and agonists should be intact. However, fine manipulations may be impaired while the co-ordination is adequate. When analysing the performances of various groups of children we did in fact find this type of relationship between co-ordination of the arms and legs and manipulative ability. Co-ordination proved to be a prerequisite for fine manipulative abilities but not the other way round. Consequently, if deficiencies exist in both, the co-ordination should be trained first (by physiotherapy) and fine manipulative abilities should be trained (by occupational therapy) only after co-ordination has clearly improved.

Difficulties in co-ordination may be due to maturational retardation, defects in the proprioceptive system (posterior tracts, cerebellum, for example), intoxications and so on. Difficulties in fine manipulative abilities may be attributed to the same causes, but may also be due to cortical dysfunction. Ingram (1967) has emphasised the incidence of hypoglycaemic attacks in infancy and childhood as an often overlooked cause of slight co-ordination difficulties. The initial signs of progressive disease may be slight disturbances of co-ordination such as difficulties in swallowing, articulation defects, unsteady gait or slight ataxia. This may be the case with cerebellar or brain stem tumours, metabolic disorders such as Hartnup disease, degenerative diseases (Friedreich's ataxia, ataxia teleangiectasia) and even disseminated sclerosis (Aigner and Siekert 1959).

Sensory Disturbances

It is well known that disturbances of vision or hearing, whether major or minor, may have profound effects on the child's learning capacities, and in recent years emphasis has been laid on the importance of detecting such defects at an early age. Slight abnormalities may remain undetected for a long time. For instance, partial deafness in which most of the sound spectrum is adequately perceived but a small part is missing may escape the attention of parents and teachers, and may result in the loss of important information for the child. Doctors should be alert to these possibilities.

The rôle of other disturbances of sensation is much less clear. In the more severely brain-damaged children, the whole field of visual perception disorders has been extensively studied (see, for example, Abercrombie's review 1964). Often it has not proved possible to distinguish between central problems of perception and the rôle of sensory loss itself. We ourselves, as mentioned previously, have found it difficult to devise adequate tests for sensory functioning, and can add little to a discussion of this topic. Minor disturbances such as slight defects in exteroceptive and proprioceptive perception may result in distorted pattern-formation in the brain. In cases of brain damage, auditory-visual interpretation and the ability to translate tactile and kinesthetic sensations into visual information, which normally develop between the ages of five and ten years, have been found to be defective (Belmont *et al.* 1966, Birch and Belmont 1965/1966, Birch and Bortner 1967). However, there is no certain direct relationship between the various kinds of visual system disorders (*e.g.* (latent) strabismus, nystagmus, unbalanced eye movements, choreiform jerks, faulty convergence, amblyopia) and complex behavioural and/or learning disorders. One of the aims of a careful descriptive examination is to be able to analyse this often too-easily assumed relationship.

Miscellaneous Signs (a Syndrome consisting of the Absence of a Syndrome)

It is evident that a considerable amount of overlap exists between the groups of signs which have been discussed so far. Indeed, it would be quite exceptional to find indications of one of these conditions without any signs that could not also belong to another group.

However, one may be confronted by a set of findings which do not show any clear relationship with one another, and from which no specific or recognisable pattern emerges. Such signs may be unequivocally and persistently present. For example, a child may show increased tendon reflexes on one side of the body, but an increased amount of associated movements on the other side; persistent infantile reflexes on the side of the increased tendon reflexes, but alterations of the footsole reflex on the other side; dominance may be very poorly expressed, and motor functions like hopping, kicking or fine finger manipulations may appear to be impaired on one or other side of the body, more or less at random.

Another example is the child who cannot tie up his shoe-laces, cannot cope with buttons, cannot ride a bicycle, *i.e.* a child who shows many insufficiencies in motor behaviour, while few marked signs of nervous dysfunction are revealed by a strict neurological examination. Walton (1963) called such children 'clumsy children' and reported very few signs of nervous dysfunction which we have discussed on neurological examination; Illingworth (1963) reported marked signs which, however, did not show the same pattern in cases with the same deficits in motor functioning.

Clearly, the opposite pattern may also be found, *i.e.* children without any motor difficulties at all may still show marked signs of nervous dysfunction which cannot be arranged into specific patterns.

The Neurological Profile

It may be useful to draw up a neurological profile, especially when minor neurological signs cannot be arranged into a pattern which allows a definite diagnosis (Fig. 55). This profile offers a quick general view of the quantitative distribution of the optimal and non-optimal signs over the subsystems of the nervous system which can be distinguished.

The composition of the subsystems is based mainly on practical clinical and/or neurophysiological consideration and these subsystems have been tested in several groups of children of varying ages with an eye to the internal consistency of the items arranged in one subsystem, and to the correlation between the various subsystems

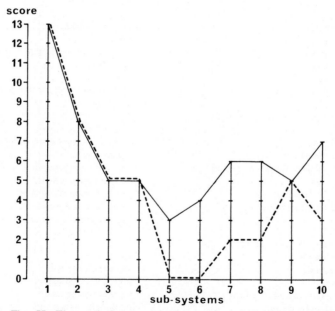

Fig. 55. The vertical represents the number of test-items scored correctly in each of the ten subsystems (numbered on the horizontal) described in Table VI. The solid line represents the highest score possible for each subsystem. The broken line represents the profile of a child with minor neurological dysfunction in fine manipulative ability (score of 0), kinesia (score of 0) and visual system (score of 3). Although gross motor functioning and motility are not optimal, associated movements are not excessive. These findings are too mild to justify a traditional diagnosis.

115

TABLE VI

Groups of items in the subsystems of the neurological profile

(1) *Sensorimotor apparatus*
 resistance to passive movement
 muscle power
 range of movements
 muscle consistency
 knee jerk
 ankle jerk
 threshold muscle reflexes (legs)
 biceps reflex
 triceps reflex
 threshold muscle reflexes (arms)
 abdominal skin reflex
 footsole reflex
 other exteroceptic reflexes (big toe)

(2) *Posture*
 sitting, general
 feet, sitting
 standing, general
 legs, standing
 feet, standing
 extended arms, standing
 walking
 lying in prone and supine position

(3) *Balance of trunk*
 response to push, standing
 following object with eyes and head
 Romberg sign
 rebound phenomenon
 walking along a straight line

(4) *Co-ordination of the extremities*
 finger-tip nose test
 diadochokinesis
 knee-heel test
 kicking against examiner's hand
 finger-tip touching test

(5) *Fine manipulative ability*
 finger-opposition test
 follow-a-finger test
 circle test

(6) *(Dys)kinesia*
 choreiform movements distal
 choreiform movements proximal
 choreiform movements during spontaneous
  behaviour
 athetotiform movements

(7) *Gross motor functions*
 heel-toe-gait during walking
 walking on tiptoe
 walking on heels
 standing on one leg
 hopping on one leg
 rising into sitting from lying
 in supine position

(8) *Quality of motility*
 speed
 smoothness }small motor movements
 adequacy
 speed
 smoothness }gross motor movements
 adequacy

(9) *Associated movements*
 mouth-opening finger-spreading
  phenomenon
 a.m. accompanying diadochokinesis
  in opposite hand
 a.m. accompanying walking on tiptoe
 a.m. accompanying walking on heels
 a.m. accompanying finger-opposition test in
  other hand

(10) *Visual system*
 position of the eyes
 directional nystagmus
 position nystagmus
 optokinetic nystagmus
 pursuit movements of the eyes
 visual fields
 funduscopy

116

themselves. Table VI lists the neurological items of the 10 subsystems. The first six, namely sensorimotor system, posture, trunk co-ordination, co-ordination of hands and feet, fine manipulative ability and the presence or absence of slight dyskinesias, are obvious entities. The distinction between sensorimotor system and posture is made for practical reasons. The sensorimotor system mainly comprises items which require manipulation of the patient, while posture consists of items which can be observed without touching him. Obviously, these subsystems are strongly inter-related. The next three subsystems, however, show a weak interrelationship but are reasonably consistent internally. The distinction between these three subsystems appears to have great practical value, especially with regard to treatment. The subsystem of dyskinesias (Group 6) consists of choreiform dyskinesia, which can be found with or without the involvement of other subsystems. (Severe dyskinesias, such as choreo-athetoses need not be considered in the profile as they can be diagnosed according to well-known classifications.) The remaining four subsystems are mainly heuristic. Actually 'gross motor functions' evaluates achievement rather than neuro-logical functioning in itself and can only be interpreted in combination with the foregoing six. Pure motor retardation, on the other hand, may manifest itself in this subsystem all by itself. The group of items 'quality of motility' describes the kind of motor behaviour which is unusual and spectacular, but it is obvious that its significance largely depends on the findings in the first six subsystems. Group 9 is added because 'associated movements' are often found in children with minor neurological dysfunction. The internal consistency of the items in these groups is low, however, (see the paragraph on associated movements) and their clinical significance is often unclear. The last group contains a more or less miscellaneous group of items concerning the visual system; they often show a low interrelationship, but they can be separated from the other neurological items by description.

Generally speaking, the profile serves two purposes. It enables the examiner to describe findings which cannot be arranged into traditional diagnostic patterns and it may visualize the occurrence in one single child of various syndromes, as described in the foregoing paragraphs. In this way it is possible to distinguish groups of children with various kinds of minor neurological dysfunction. Subsequently, an attempt can be made to establish relationships between these findings and other objective evaluations of the child's behavioural condition.

CHAPTER 13

The Relationship between Minor Neurological Dysfunction and Behaviour

Since behaviour is a manifestation of brain activity, the question is whether aberrant behaviour can be traced back to specific dysfunctions of the brain. In this context, a dysfunction of the brain is inferred from evidence found during the neurological examination. This statement gives rise to another question: is it only from evidence found at the neurological examination that one can infer that the brain is impaired? Evidently not. It is well-known that lesions of the brain (even the larger ones, such as frontal lobe tumours) may sometimes pass unobserved, with no neurological signs found at the neurological assessment and with no recognised behavioural alterations over a long period of time. Still, one can maintain that any behaviour—adequate or inadequate—is mediated by the brain. Aberrant behaviour, therefore, can be found while there is no evidence of brain dysfunction; it is also possible that definite signs of brain impairment may be found while there is no disrupted behaviour. How can this seemingly inextricable problem be solved?

In the first place, it should be realised that brain activity (activity determining complex behaviour) is determined by the natural history of the brain. In this, two factors play a decisive rôle: the first is the superabundance of neurons with their possible interconnections formed in accordance with the genetic blueprint of the individual brain. Secondly, there is the personal experience of the individual, steering which neurons become operational and probably also the structural formation of the neuronal connections established during development (Braitenberg 1977). As neither the genetic blueprint nor the personal experience of two individuals are ever the same, no two brains will be completely similar. As a result, we are confronted with varying behaviours generated by varying brains.

In the second place, behaviour, and especially complex behaviour, is also environmentally dependent, in the sense that a particular behaviour can be considered inadequate in one situation while it may be acceptable in another. Moreover, interaction with the environment affects the composition of the behaviour, and thus the way in which the brain generates the behaviour. Consequently, it must be possible to create specific 'positive' environmental conditions in which a brain functions adequately, while the same brain functions inadequately in other 'negative' environments. This implies that even morphologically (and therefore functionally) damaged brains may produce socially acceptable 'normal' behaviour in specific environmental conditions, while, as is well known, even 'normal' brains may show a wide variety of behaviour under extreme conditions.

As for our original question—whether aberrant behaviour can be traced back to specific dysfunctions of the brain—the answer will be yes and no, depending on the type of behaviour and the type of brain dysfunction of the child in question, *and* on the possibility of appreciating the *variability* in brain activity and environmental conditions of that particular child. This factor—the variability—should be considered an important co-determinant in the study of brain-behaviour relationships.

It is not surprising, therefore, that the two approaches to the study of disturbed behaviour in relation to brain damage mentioned in Chapter 2 (either selecting children with disturbed behaviour and trying to find a connection with neurological dysfunction, or selecting neurologically impaired children and studying their behaviour) produce variable results. With the exception of extreme conditions (such as severe brain trauma causing comatose states, or extensive brain lesions causing spastic tetraplegia), one may hardly expect to find uniform relationships. It is also clear how fruitless it would be to look for a common aetiology for the heterogeneous group of so-called MBD children. As a general conclusion at this point, it must be said that the question of a possible 'organic basis' underlying particular behavioural and/or learning difficulties (see Chapter 1) is the wrong question. All behaviour has an organic basis. The absence of signs of neurological dysfunction does not prove that there is no brain dysfunction underlying a behavioural disturbance, while the presence of both minor neurological dysfunction and behavioural and learning difficulties does not mean that naturally these two are causally related.

The analysis of behavioural disturbance is the analysis of a very complex function of the nervous system. Such an analysis must be carried out using appropriate instruments, the neurological examination being one only and referring to a limited part of complex behaviour. The other instruments comprise neuropsychological and observational methods (for free-field behaviour see Kalverboer 1975). The way in which the results of the neurological examination may contribute to the analysis of the behavioural disorder in a particular child should now be assessed.

In some cases one may contend that the neurological condition has had a distinct part in the genesis of particular aspects of the behaviour; sometimes even a causal relationship may be assumed to exist, although such a relationship would not explain the total behaviour of the child. A patient with mild co-ordination difficulties or manipulative disabilities may show an impairment of all the behaviour patterns requiring fine motor manipulation, thus he will be handicapped in his everyday behaviour. Each child will react to this sort of handicap in an individual way, depending on the number of other variables which have to be assessed. A child with marked choreiform jerks in the eye muscles may appear to be deficient in those behaviour patterns which require steady fixation, but the degree of handicap will depend on many other factors. Paroxysmal epileptic activity in the brain, resulting in a cessation of function, will interrupt continuous performances, but in such patients there are also other factors which determine the final behaviour of the child in his attempts to compensate for his handicap.

On the other hand, a direct relationship between signs of neurological dysfunction and even a part of the behavioural disturbance shown cannot often be implied. It is difficult to see how an asymmetrical abdominal skin reflex, a slight difference in the resistance to passive movements or slight asymmetry in the intensity of the tendon reflexes may result in specific, disturbed behaviour. Obviously, in such cases a causal relationship is improbable, although possibly the neurological findings reflect changes in the organisation of the brain which may manifest themselves in the behavioural dimension as well, since both sets of findings (the behavioural and the neurological) originate from the same source. This point cannot be proved irrefutably; however, a few hypotheses can be drawn up of which the value has to be tested in each case:

A. It is a reasonable assumption that neurological signs reflect a brain dysfunction, and that often this dysfunction is caused by a brain lesion (which need not be unifocal or strictly localised). But a brain lesion must not be looked on as a static condition. It is well known that there are several morphological compensatory mechanisms which may succeed in restructuring the brain. This has been observed in various animal species, often with striking differences between the infant and adult animal. Prechtl (1978) has published an extensive review and discussion on this issue and has concluded that there are sufficient indications to support the idea that similar mechanisms may be active in man. He suggests that via the several morphological compensatory mechanisms, a brain, when structurally damaged at an early age, may grow into a different brain, which means that "infants who acquire brain damage may develop a brain which is biologically different from the normally developing brain" (Prechtl 1978). This is in fact an enlargement of what has been said at the beginning of this chapter, namely, that the development of the brain depends on both innate capacities and environmental, personal experience; in the event of the brain becoming damaged, a considerable degree of 'rewiring' may occur.

Thus, in some children who show a neurological dysfunction the rewiring of the brain may have been inadequate, which results in particular aberrant behaviour in particular circumstances. In its extreme consequence the rewiring may bring about a condition in which there are no persisting neurological defects, but in which only some peculiar types of behaviour indicate a biologically different, even aberrantly wired, brain. This hypothesis of the rewiring of the damaged nervous system is very attractive as it explains part of the variety of forms of behaviour which can be found in children with so-called MBD.

B. Another hypothesis about the relation between neurological dysfunction and behaviour is based on the concept of variability being a characteristic of the healthy brain, and of the decrease in this variability in the case of brain dysfunction (Touwen 1976, 1978a, 1978b). In this context, the term variability is used for the intrinsic ability of the brain—due to the superabundance of neuronal connections—to reach goals (e.g. walking, grasping or more complex skills) in various ways, that is, by the use of various strategies at different times. Minor or major neurological dysfunction is characterised by a decrease in this variability; the number of strategies is reduced as a result of the brain lesion. The decrease in variability results in stereotyped performances (which can be distorted, as in cerebral palsy for instance), rigid stimulus-response relationships (stereotyped reflexes for instance) and in a lack of adaptability to the varying demands of the environment.

At first glance this seems to be in contradiction to the unpredictable and highly variable behavioural symptomatology of the so-called MBD children. However, the main point is whether the behavioural symptomatology is really so variable and unpredictable intra-individually, or whether it is in fact relatively stereotyped, being variable and unpredictable only in appearance because it does not come into the category of expected 'normal' behaviour (which inter-individually may be quite variable).

Let us for a moment reflect on the process of functional brain development. One of the ways in which it can be elucidated is by reference to Sir Karl Popper's problem-solving theory (Popper 1972, Popper and Eccles 1977), whereby problem solving is carried out by trial, followed by error elimination. A hypothesis for the solution to a problem is drawn up, tested and then reformulated, the errors which have become evident during the test-trials being taken into account. Renewed testing may result in the discovery of new errors, which have to be eliminated by a further refinement of the hypothetical solution of the problem. This process continues until the best solution to the problem is found. As Popper has pointed out, functional brain development can be regarded as a continuous process of problem solving, starting from innate dispositions. The brain has to meet the various and increasingly complex demands of the environment; in its attempt to do so it builds up hypotheses which are tested to evaluate their adequacy. On the basis of the test results new hypotheses are formed and the error elimination is applied over and over again. This process is feasible because, as it develops, the brain can make use of an increasingly complex neuronal wiring system with increasing capacities. Because no two demands of the environment are identical, and there is a superabundance of neuronal connections in the healthy brain, during development the brain builds up a large set of strategies with which to meet the continually changing demands of the environment.

In the case of brain dysfunction, the brain may not be so well equipped for this developmental process and this may be evident in various ways. First, the brain may not be able to apply varying modes of operation in different situations, due to the lack of adequate 'hardware': it has to apply one and the same mode for solving a variety of problems, which results in stereotyped and often inadequate behaviour. This behaviour may appear to be unexpected as it falls outside the range of expected behaviour. An extreme example of this phenomenon is the temper tantrum, which can be seen as a primitive form of coping with otherwise unsolvable problems. As we know, in children with behavioural difficulties temper tantrums often occur without any apparent immediate cause. This may be explained by the fact that an unsolvable problem for the child is not even perceived as a problem by the adult and the child's behaviour may therefore seem inadequate and unpredictable to the adult.

Secondly, in children with neurological dysfunction the process of trial and elimination of error may last longer than in normal children. Due to the deficiency in the 'hardware' of the nervous system, the best 'programme' to be used for the problem in question is not easily found and many trials have to be made. Meanwhile, the child grows older and his brain attains a high degree of structural complexity. This may lead to pseudo-infantile behaviour since some aspects of the child's behaviour are in accordance with the more complex brain specific for his age and some aspects may appear to belong to a lower age-range. The combination may easily give the impression of age-inadequate and unusual behaviour, which may vary according to the environmental demands.

121

Thirdly, in the case of neurological dysfunction, the brain may be completely unable to find the proper solution for its task requirements due to its limited potentiality. It has to take refuge in less adequate or inappropriate modes of operation in order to meet the demands of the environment. One may call this 'substitution', but it is sometimes a deficient substitution and results in unusual and unexpected behaviour.

Finally, errors sometimes remain in spite of (or even because of) frantic attempts at trial and elimination of error. The brain may also not even recognise the errors, although they keep recurring, because of a lack of functioning feed-back systems. Such errors may explain some of the strange, often inadequate and unpredictable reactions of children with behavioural difficulties. The reactions themselves may be stereotyped in relation to the environmental events by which they are provoked, but their distribution over time may be as unpredictable as the events themselves.

It is obvious that the possibilities which are discussed here are not mutually exclusive and that there is a wide overlap and intricate relationship between them. This hypothesis may explain part of the behavioural difficulty of a child with evidence of a (minor) neurological dysfunction (MND). It implies possibilities for treatment, which mainly consist of inventing ways to help the child overcome his behavioural difficulties by improving his trial and error elimination in specific situations (Touwen 1978a).

Finally, what are the conclusions and what are the perspectives? First, it must be stressed that terms like MBD and MND are misleading in that they suggest a diagnosis. At the most they can be considered as global indicators of the need for a careful and comprehensive examination (both from the behavioural and neurological points of view) in order to arrive at a specific diagnosis. The term MBD used as a diagnostic category is erroneous. MND as a general description must be specified, because in itself it is deficient.

In the second place, a simple and direct relationship between behavioural disorders and neurological impairment cannot be expected except in rare cases. A careful analysis is always required to find out how, and to what extent, behavioural and neurological symptoms are related. The results of this analysis may suggest some forms of treatment.

In the third place, it is essential to recognise the significance of the variability of brains resulting in the variability of behaviour as an important co-determinant of neurobehavioural relationships. It is interesting to study variability as a separate factor because it is probably the main cause of the variance found in the relationships between neurological dysfunction and behaviour. Several aspects of this variable can be distinguished. There is the intra-individual variability of the healthy brain, and the decrease in this variability with brain dysfunction. There is the variability of the different brains themselves, due to inter-individual differences in genetic blueprint and personal experience. There is the variability between brains with brain damage, due to individual differences in compensation mechanisms and the subsequent 'rewiring' of the brain. Then there is the variability of environmental conditions, inter- as well as intra-individually—in one place (at home) or in different places (at home and at school), displayed by one person (the mother) or different persons (the mother, father, teacher and so on)—and its effect on brain development and brain functioning.

We know little about the effect of these kinds of variability on the development of the brain and its functioning, yet their importance cannot be overrated. It may be that for one particular brain one particular environment is optimal and has to be chosen from a variety of possible environments, or it has to be actively produced by the brain itself in its interaction with the environment. It is possible that the inability to choose and produce the optimal environment is one of the main problems of the dysfunctioning brain. This may result in a spiralling of difficulties, because functioning in the wrong environment may cause inadequate brain activity which, in its turn, will result in repercussions from the environment and so on. The influence of inter-individual variability must also be studied in order to recognise the complexity of the neurobehavioural relationship and help the brain to choose and to produce. One might say that in the development of neurobehavioural relationships the signal-noise ratio (to borrow a term from information theory) is a strong determinant for the type of behaviour which will arise. It is a case of a signal-noise ratio in which the noise does not merely blur the signal but also affects it. We often know a great deal about the signal. We must find out more about the noise.

NOTES

Examination Proforma for Minor Neurological Dysfunction

'State' and 'Social Responsiveness' are scored at each stage of the examination and any change in either should be scored in the column opposite the test in which the change occurred.

Unless otherwise indicated, the scoring on the left side of the proforma applies to the left side of the body, and that on the right to the right side of the body.

ASSESSMENT OF SITTING

			State	Soc. Resp.

Spontaneous Motility

Quantity	gross movements	0 1 2 3		
	small movements	0 1 2 3		
Quality	speed	0 1 2 3		
	smoothness	0 1 2 3		
	adequacy	0 1 2 3		

Involuntary Movements

absent
present (describe)

Posture

Head	0 1 2	rotated	0 1 2
	0 1 2	bent laterally	0 1 2
(ante)	0 1 2	flexion	0 1 2 (retro)
Trunk	0 1 2	rotated	0 1 2
	0 1 2	bent laterally	0 1 2
	0 1 2	kyphosis	0 1 2
	0 1 2	lordosis	0 1 2
	symmetrically collapsed		0 1 2
Legs	0 1 2	endorotation	0 1 2
	0 1 2	exorotation	0 1 2
	0 1 2	flexion	0 1 2
	0 1 2	extension	0 1 2
	0 1 2	adduction	0 1 2
	0 1 2	abduction	0 1 2
Feet	0 1 2	endorotation	0 1 2
	0 1 2	exorotation	0 1 2
	0 1 2	dorsiflexion	0 1 2
	0 1 2	plantar flexion	0 1 2
	0 1 2	adduction	0 1 2
	0 1 2	abduction	0 1 2

Reaction to Push against Shoulder

0 1 2 3	balance	0 1 2 3

Following an Object

0 1 2 3	balance and rotation	0 1 2 3

125

EXAMINATION OF THE MOTOR SYSTEM

					State	Soc. Resp.

Muscle Power

0	1	2	3	neck	0	1	2	3
0	1	2	3	shoulders	0	1	2	3
0	1	2	3	elbows	0	1	2	3
0	1	2	3	wrists	0	1	2	3
0	1	2	3	hands	0	1	2	3
0	1	2	3	hips*	0	1	2	3
0	1	2	3	knees	0	1	2	3
0	1	2	3	ankles	0	1	2	3
0	1	2	3	feet	0	1	2	3

Resistance to Passive Movements

0	1	2	3	neck	0	1	2	3
0	1	2	3	shoulders	0	1	2	3
0	1	2	3	elbows	0	1	2	3
0	1	2	3	wrists	0	1	2	3
0	1	2	3	hands	0	1	2	3
0	1	2	3	hips*	0	1	2	3
0	1	2	3	knees	0	1	2	3
0	1	2	3	ankles	0	1	2	3
0	1	2	3	feet	0	1	2	3

Range of Movements**

Head anteflexion
 retroflexion
 rotation

Shoulder abduction
 circumduction of arm

Elbow extension
 flexion

Wrists hyper-extension
 flexion

Hips abduction
 circumduction of leg

Knees extension
 flexion

Ankles dorsiflexion
 plantar flexion
 rotation

Kicking

0	1	2	3	median	0	1	2	3
0	1	2	3	45° inwards	0	1	2	3
0	1	2	3	45° outwards	0	1	2	3

total score

*For practical reasons the results of the examination of the hips are recorded here, although the examination itself is carried out at a later stage of the procedure.

**Deviations from the average range of movements described in the text should be recorded as quantitatively as possible.

EXAMINATION OF REFLEXES

							State	Soc. Resp.

Tendon Reflexes

0	1	2	3	4	ankle jerk	0	1	2	3	4
0	1	2	3		threshold	0	1	2	3	
0	1	2	3		ankle clonus	0	1	2	3	
0	1	2	3	4	knee jerk	0	1	2	3	4
0	1	2	3		threshold	0	1	2	3	
0	1	2	3		biceps reflex	0	1	2	3	
0	1	2	3		threshold	0	1	2	3	
0	1	2	3		triceps reflex	0	1	2	3	
0	1	2	3		threshold	0	1	2	3	

Plantar Response

Big Toe	0	1	2	dorsiflexion	0	1	2	
	0	1	2	plantar flexion	0	1	2	
Other	0	1		fanning	0	1		
Toes	0	1	2	plantar grasp	0	1	2	

Other Reflexes

0	1	2	3	palmo-mental reflex	0	1	2	3
0	1	2		Mayer reflex	0	1	2	
0	1	2		Léri reflex	0	1	2	

ASSESSMENT OF STANDING

		State	Soc. Resp.

Posture

Head	0	1	2	rotated	0	1	2	
	0	1	2	bent laterally	0	1	2	
(ante)	0	1	2	flexion	0	1	2	(retro)

Trunk	0	1	2	rotated	0	1	2	
	0	1	2	bent laterally	0	1	2	
	0	1	2	kyphosis	0	1	2	
	0	1	2	lordosis	0	1	2	
				symmetrically collapsed	0	1	2	
				left shoulder lower than right: no, yes	cm			
				right shoulder lower than left: no, yes	cm			

Upper Limbs	0	1	2	endorotation	0	1	2	
	0	1	2	exorotation	0	1	2	
	0	1	2	flexion	0	1	2	
	0	1	2	extension	0	1	2	
	0	1	2	adduction	0	1	2	
	0	1	2	abduction	0	1	2	

Pelvis	left crista iliaca lower than right: no, yes cm
	right crista iliaca lower than left: no, yes cm

Legs	0	1	2	endorotation	0	1	2
	0	1	2	exorotation	0	1	2
	0	1	2	flexion	0	1	2
	0	1	2	extension	0	1	2
	0	1	2	adduction	0	1	2
	0	1	2	abduction	0	1	2
Feet	0	1	2	endorotation	0	1	2
	0	1	2	exorotation	0	1	2
	0	1	2	flexion	0	1	2
	0	1	2	extension	0	1	2
	0	1	2	adduction	0	1	2
	0	1	2	abduction	0	1	2

Arch of the Foot   left   cm. (without correction of
                                                    ankle position)
                        right   cm.
                        left   cm. (after correction of
                                                    ankle position)
                        right   cm.

pes planus:
pes excavatus:
distance between feet for balance:

Spontaneous Motility

Quantity	gross movements	0	1	2	3
	small movements	0	1	2	3
Quality	speed	0	1	2	3
	smoothness	0	1	2	3
	adequacy	0	1	2	3

Involuntary Movements

absent
present (describe)

Pronation of Arms (20sec)

0	1	2	spooning	0	1	2
0	1	2	deviation from median line	0	1	2
0			deviation from horizontal	0		

Supination of Arms (20sec)

0	1	2	pronation	0	1	2

TESTS FOR INVOLUNTARY MOVEMENTS (20sec)

0	1	2	3	distal choreiform movements	0	1	2	3
0	1	2	3	proximal choreiform movements	0	1	2	3
0	1	2	3	athetotiform movements	0	1	2	3

State	*Soc. Resp.*

128

0	1	2	3	choreatic movements	0	1	2	3
0	1	2	3	athetotic movements	0	1	2	3
0	1	2	3	tremor	0	1	2	3

TESTS FOR CO-ORDINATION AND ASSOCIATED MOVEMENTS

0	1	2	3	mouth-opening finger-spreading phenomenon	0	1	2	3
0	1	2	3	diadochokinesis	0	1	2	3
0	1	2	3	associated movements	0	1	2	3

(diadochokinesis of right hand)　　　　　　(diadochokinesis of left hand)

Finger-nose Test

Eyes open

0	1	2	tremor	0	1	2
0	1	2	touching nose correctly	0	1	2
yes		no	consistent deviation to left	yes		no
yes		no	consistent deviation to right	yes		no

Eyes closed

0	1	2	tremor	0	1	2
0	1	2	touching nose correctly	0	1	2
yes		no	consistent deviation to left	yes		no
yes		no	consistent deviation to right	yes		no

Fingertip-touching Test

Eyes open

0	1	2	tremor during movement	0	1	2
0	1	2	tremor in placed finger	0	1	2
0	1	2	placing finger correctly	0	1	2
yes		no	consistent deviation to left	yes		no
yes		no	consistent deviation to right	yes		no

Eyes closed

0	1	2	tremor during movement	0	1	2
0	1	2	tremor in placed finger	0	1	2
0	1	2	placing finger correctly	0	1	2
yes		no	consistent deviation to left	yes		no
yes		no	consistent deviation to right	yes		no

Finger Opposition Test

0	1	2	smoothness	0	1	2
0	1	2	finger-to-finger transition	0	1	2
0	1	2	mirror movements	0	1	2

State ／ *Soc. Resp.*

129

Follow-a-Finger Test

0	1	2	smoothness	0	1	2

Circle Test

0	1	2	mirror	0	1	2
0	1	2	unidirectional	0	1	2
0	1	2	transition	0	1	2

Standing with Eyes Closed

balance   0   1   2   3

tendency to fall consistently to the left, right side.

Reaction to Push against Shoulder

0   1   2   3   balance   0   1   2   3

	State	Soc. Resp.

ASSESSMENT OF WALKING

Posture

Head

0	1	2	rotated	0	1	2	
0	1	2	bent laterally	0	1	2	
(ante) 0	1	2	flexed	0	1	2	(retro)

Trunk

0	1	2	rotated	0	1	2
0	1	2	bent laterally	0	1	2
0	1	2	kyphosis	0	1	2
0	1	2	lordosis	0	1	2
		symmetrically collapsed	0	1	2	

Arms

0	1	2	endorotation	0	1	2
0	1	2	exorotation	0	1	2
0	1	2	flexion	0	1	2
0	1	2	extension	0	1	2
0	1	2	adduction	0	1	2
0	1	2	abduction	0	1	2

Gait

			width (constancy)	0	1		
			(measurement)	0	1	2	3
0	1	2	circumduction	0	1	2	
0	1	2	movements of pelvis	0	1	2	
0	1	2	movements of knees	0	1	2	
0	1	2	heel-toe gait	0	1	2	
0	1	2	3 arm movements	0	1	2	3

Placing of Feet

0	1	2	abduction	0	1	2
0	1	2	adduction	0	1	2
0	1	2	dorsiflexion	0	1	2
0	1	2	plantar flexion	0	1	2
0	1	2	on medial side	0	1	2
0	1	2	on lateral side	0	1	2

Walking along a Straight Line

0   1   2   3   4   deviations   0   1   2   3   4

Other Gross Motor Functions

		0	1	2	3	walking on tiptoe	0	1	2	3		
		0	1	2	3	associated movements	0	1	2	3		
		0	1	2	3	walking on heels	0	1	2	3		
		0	1	2	3	associated movements	0	1	2	3		
0 1 2	3 4	5	6			standing on one leg	0	1	2	3	4 5	6
0 1 2	3 4	5	6			hopping	0	1	2	3	4 5	6

ASSESSMENT OF THE TRUNK (STANDING)

Inspection of the Back and Spine

0 = normal   5 = operation scars
1 = slight hairiness   6 = lipomas
2 = tufts of hair   7 = café-au-lait spots
3 = cutaneous dimples 8 = other (describe)
4 = sinus opening

scoliosis to left	0 1 2
scoliosis to right	0 1 2
kyphosis	0 1 2
lordosis	0 1 2
limitation of movements:	no
	yes (describe)

Skin Reflexes

Abdominal skin reflex:

0	1	2	supra-umbilical	0 1 2
0	1	2	umbilical	0 1 2
0	1	2	infra-umbilical	0 1 2
0	1	2	cremasteric reflex	0 1 2
0	1	2	Galant response	0 1 2

ASSESSMENT OF LYING

Prone

Spine   0   1   2   scoliosis   0   1   2

processi spinosi   present
                   absent (describe)

limitation of movement   no
                         yes (describe)

For examination of hip joints, see page 126 of Proforma.

Posture of Legs and Feet in Prone Position

0	1	2	abduction	0 1 2
0	1	2	adduction	0 1 2
0	1	2	flexion	0 1 2
0	1	2	extension	0 1 2
0	1	2	exorotation	0 1 2
0	1	2	endorotation	0 1 2

State	*Soc. Resp.*

131

Posture of Legs and Feet in Supine Position

0	1	2	abduction	0	1	2
0	1	2	adduction	0	1	2
0	1	2	flexion	0	1	2
0	1	2	extension	0	1	2
0	1	2	exorotation	0	1	2
0	1	2	endorotation	0	1	2

Knee-heel Test

0	1	2	accurate placing	0	1	2
0	1	2	sliding heel	0	1	2

Sitting up Without Help of Hands   0   1   2

ASSESSMENT OF THE HEAD

Facial Musculature

0	1	2	at rest	0	1	2
0	1	2	voluntary movements	0	1	2
0	1	2	emotional movements	0	1	2

Position of Eyes

no strabismus and no heterophoria
no strabismus, heterophoria

exophoria	left
exophoria	right
hyperphoria	both
hypophoria	

concomitant strabismus

convergent	left
divergent	right
other	both

non-concomitant strabismus (describe)

Fixation

deviation: no
                         left, type:
                         right, type:
                         both, type:

choreiform movements: absent
                         present

manifest strabismus: absent
                         present, type:

Pursuit Movements

range of movements: intact
                         deviant (describe)

choreiform movements: absent
                         present

ataxic eye movements: absent
                         present

manifest strabismus: absent
                         present, type:

imbalance: absent
                         present

State	Soc. Resp.

132

Convergence

left eye	0	1	2
right eye	0	1	2

pupillary reaction: absent
                           present

Nystagmus

spontaneous nystagmus: absent
                           present

direction:
intensity:
directional nystagmus: absent
                           present

direction:
intensity:

Optokinetic Nystagmus   symmetrical
                                  asymmetrical
                                  vertical
                                  horizontal

Pupillary Reactions

direct:	0	1	2
indirect:	0	1	2

Visual Acuity

normal
abnormal (specify)

Visual Field

normal
abnormal (specify)

Choreiform Movements of the Face   absent
                                                        present

Ears

0	1	2	low voice	0	1	2
0	1	2	localisation of sound	0	1	2

Tongue

motility: smooth
                 awkward

choreiform movements: absent
                           present

fasciculations: absent
                     present

Pharyngeal Arches   symmetrical
                          asymmetrical
                          (describe)

Spontaneous Motility   decreased
                          the same
                          increased

Funduscopy   normal
                     abnormal (specify)

133

General Data

height:

weight:

circumference of skull:

abnormalities of skull:

general paediatric data:

preference of hands: right, left, both

preference of feet: right, left, both

preference of eyes: right, left, both

fine motor coordination in manipulation:

tactile sensation:

pain:

temperature:

kinesthesia:

sense of position:

dermographia:

speech:

NOTES

NOTES

REFERENCES

Abercrombie, M. L. J., Lindon, R. L., Tyson, M. C. (1964) 'Associated movements in normal and physically handicapped children.' *Developmental Medicine and Child Neurology,* **6,** 573-580.

Abrams, A. L. (1968) 'Delayed irregular maturation versus minimal brain injury. Recommendations for a change in current nomenclature.' *Clinical Pediatrics,* **7,** 344-349.

Adams, R. M., Kocsis, J. S., Estes, R. E. (1974) 'Soft neurological signs in learning-disabled children and controls.' *American Journal of Diseases of Children,* **128,** 614-618.

Aigner, B. R., Siekert, R. G. (1959) 'Differential diagnosis of acute ataxia in children.' *Proceedings of the Staff Meetings of the Mayo Clinic,* **34,** 573-581.

André-Thomas, S., Chesni, Y., Saint-Anne Dargassies, S. (1960) *The Neurological Examination of the Infant. Little Club Clinics in Developmental Medicine, No. 1.* Spastics Society with Heinemann.

Arnold, L. E. (1973) 'Is this label necessary?' *Journal of School Health,* **43,** 510-514.

—— (1976) 'Minimal brain dysfunction: a hydraulic parfait model.' *Diseases of the Nervous System,* **37,** 171-176.

Barlow, C. F. (1974) '"Soft signs" in children with learning disorders.' *American Journal of Diseases of Children,* **128,** 605-606.

Bax, M., Mac Keith, R. (1963) *Minimal Cerebral Dysfunction. Clinics in Developmental Medicine, No. 10.* London: Spastics Society with Heinemann.

Becker, R. D. (1976) 'The neurology of childhood learning disorders: the minimal brain dysfunction syndrome re-examined.' *Therapeutic Education,* **4,** 20-31.

Belmont, I., Birch, H. G., Karp, E. (1966) 'The disordering of intersensory and intrasensory integration by brain damage.' *Journal of Nervous and Mental Disease,* **141,** 410-418.

Bergès, J., Lézine, I. (1965) *The Imitation of Gestures. Clinics in Developmental Medicine, No. 18.* London: Spastics Society with Heinemann.

Birch, H. G. (1964) *Brain Damage in Children.* Baltimore: Williams & Wilkins.

—— Belmont, I. (1965) 'Auditory-visual integration in brain-damaged and normal children.' *Developmental Medicine and Child Neurology,* **7,** 135-144.

—— —— (1966) 'Development and disturbance in auditory visual integration.' *Ear, Eye, Nose, and Throat Digest,* **28,** 47.

—— Bortner, M. (1967) 'Stimulus competition and concept utilization in brain damaged children.' *Developmental Medicine and Child Neurology,* **9,** 402-410.

—— Thomas, A., Chess, S. (1964) 'Behavioral development in brain damaged children.' *Archives of General Psychiatry,* **11,** 596-603.

Braitenberg, V. (1977) *On the Texture of Brains.* Berlin: Springer.

Connolly, K., Stratton, P. (1968) 'Developmental changes in associated movements.' *Developmental Medicine and Child Neurology,* **10,** 49-56.

Eisenberg, L. (1957) 'Psychiatric implications of brain damage in children.' *Psychiatric Quarterly,* **31,** 72-92.

Fog, E., Fog, M. (1963) 'Cerebral inhibition examined by associated movements.' *in* Bax, M., Mac Keith, R. (Eds.) *Minimal Cerebral Dysfunction, Clinics in Developmental Medicine, No. 10.* London: Spastics Society with Heinemann. p. 52-57.

Gellis, S. S. (1975) 'Editorial comment.' *American Journal of Diseases of Children,* **129,** 1324.

Geschwind, N. (1974) 'Late changes in the nervous system: an overview.' *in* Stein, D. G., Rosen, J. J., Butters, N. (Eds.) *Plasticity and Recovery of Function in the Central Nervous System.* New York: Academic Press. pp. 467-508.

Goldstein, K. (1936) 'Modifications of behavior consequent to cerebral lesions.' *Psychiatric Quarterly,* **10,** 589-610.

Gomez, M. R. (1967) 'Minimal cerebral dysfunction (maximal neurologic confusion).' *Clinical Pediatrics,* **6,** 589-591.

Hart, Z., Rennick, P. M., Klinge, V., Schwartz, M. L. (1974) 'A pediatric neurologist's contribution to evaluations of school underachievers.' *American Journal of Diseases of Children,* **128,** 319-323.

Holt, K. S. (1965) *Assessment of Cerebral Palsy.* London: Lloyd-Luke.

Hopkins, J. B. (1976) *A Comparative Study of Sensorimotor Development During the First Six Months of Life.* Thesis, University of Leeds.

Illingworth, R. S. (1963) 'The clumsy child.' *in* Bax, M., Mac Keith, R. (Eds.) *Minimal Cerebral Dysfunction. Clinics in Developmental Medicine, No. 10.* London: Spastics Society with Heinemann. p. 26-27.

Ingram, T. T. S., Stark, G. D., Blackburn, I. (1967) 'Ataxia and other neurological disorders as sequels of severe hypoglycaemia in childhood.' *Brain,* **90,** 851-862.

Kalverboer, A. F. (1975) *A Neurobehavioural Study in Pre-school Children. Clinics in Developmental Medicine, No. 54.* London: S.I.M.P. with Heinemann.

—— (1978) 'MBD: discussion of the concept.' *Advances in Biological Psychiatry,* **1,** 5-17.

Kiphard, E. J., Schilling, F. (1970) 'Der Hamm-Marburger Körperkoordinations-test für Kinder.' *Monatschrift für Kinderheilkunde,* **118,** 473-479.

McMahon, S. A., Greenberg, L. M. (1977) 'Serial neurological examination of hyperactive children.' *Pediatrics,* **59,** 584-587.

Mangold, B. (1974) 'Psychische Probleme beim Minimal-Brain Dysfunktion-Syndrom.' *Pädiatrie und Pädologie,* **9,** 95-103.

Munsat, T. L., Pearson, C. M. (1967) 'The differential diagnosis of neuromuscular weakness in infancy and childhood. I. Non-dystrophic disorders.' *Developmental Medicine and Child Neurology,* **9,** 220-230.

O'Malley, J. E., Eisenberg, L. (1973) 'The hyperkinetic syndrome.' *Seminars in Psychiatry,* **5,** 95-104.

Paine, R. S. (1966) 'Neurological grand rounds: minimal chronic brain syndromes.' *Clinical Proceedings of the Children's Hospital, Washington, D.C.,* **22,** 21-40.

—— Oppé, T. E. (1966) *Neurological Examination of Children. Clinics in Developmental Medicine, Nos. 20/21.* London: Spastics Society with Heinemann.

—— Werry, J. S., Quay, H. C. (1968) 'A study of "minimal brain dysfunction".' *Developmental Medicine and Child Neurology,* **10,** 505-520.

Pond, D. (1960) 'Is there a syndrome of 'brain damage' in children?' *Cerebral Palsy Bulletin,* **2,** 296-297.

Popper, K. R. (1972) *Objective Knowledge: An Evolutionary Approach.* Oxford: The Clarendon Press.

—— Eccles, J. C. (1977) *The Self and its Brain.* Berlin: Springer.

Prechtl, H. F. R. (1965) 'Prognostic value of neurological signs in the newborn infant.' *Proceedings of the Royal Society of Medicine,* **58,** 3-4.

—— (1968) 'Neurological findings in newborn infants after pre- and paranatal complications.' *in* Jonxis, J. H. P., Visser, H. K. A., Troelstra, J. A. (Eds.) *Aspects of Praematurity and Dysmaturity.* Leiden: Stenfert Kroese, p. 303.

—— (1977) *The Neurological Examintion of the Full-term Newborn Infant. 2nd edn. Clinics in Developmental Medicine, No. 63.* London: S.I.M.P. with Heinemann.

—— (1978) 'Minimal brain dysfunction syndrome and the plasticity of the nervous system.' *Advances in Biological Psychiatry,* **1,** 96-105.

—— Lenard, H. G. (1968) 'Verhalensphysiologie des Neugeborenen.' *in* Linneweh, F. (Ed.) *Fortschritte Pädologie.* Berlin: Springer. pp. 88-122.

—— Stemmer, C. (1962) 'The choreiform syndrome in children.' *Developmental Medicine and Child Neurology,* **4,** 199-227.

Robson, P. (1968) 'Persisting head-turning in the early months: some effects in the early years.' *Developmental Medicine and Child Neurology,* **10,** 82-92.

Rutter, M. (1977) 'Brain damage syndromes in childhood: concepts and findings.' *Journal of Child Psychology and Psychiatry,* **18,** 1-21.

—— Graham, P., Birch, H. G. (1966) 'Interrelations between the choreiform syndrome, reading disability and psychiatric disorder in children of 8-11 years.' *Developmental Medicine and Child Neurology,* **8,** 149-159.

—— —— Yule, W. (1970) *A Neuropsychiatric Study in Childhood. Clinics in Developmental Medicine, Nos. 35/36.* London: S.I.M.P. with Heinemann.

138

—— Yule, W. (1975) 'The concept of specific reading retardation.' *Journal of Child Psychology and Psychiatry,* **16,** 181-197.

Sainz, A. (1966) 'Hyperkinetic disease of children: diagnosis and therapy.' *Diseases of the Nervous System,* **27,** 48-50.

Sameroff, A. J., Chandler, M. J. (1975) 'Reproductive risk and the continuum of caretaking casualty.' *in* Horowitz, F. D., Hetherington, M., Scarr-Salapatek, S., Siegel, G. (Eds.) *Review of Child Development Research, Vol. 4.* Chicago: University of Chicago Press. pp. 187-244.

Satterfield, J. H., Cantwell, D. P., Lesser, L. I., Podosin, R. L. (1972) 'Physiological studies of the hyperkinetic child. I.' *American Journal of Psychiatry,* **128,** 1418-1424.

Satz, P., Rardin, D., Ross, J. (1971) 'An evaluation of a theory of specific developmental dyslexia.' *Child Development,* **42,** 2009-2021.

Schain, R. J. (1972) *Neurology of Childhood Learning Disorders.* Baltimore: Williams & Wilkins.

Schulman, J. L., Kaspar, J. C., Throne, F. M. (1965) *Brain Damage and Behavior.* Springfield, Ill.: C. C. Thomas.

Shaffer, D. (1978) 'Natural history of the minimal brain dysfunction syndrome.' *Advances in Biological Psychiatry,* **1,** 18-34.

—— McNamara, N., Pincus, J. H. (1974) 'Controlled observations on patterns of activity, attention, and impulsivity in brain-damaged and psychiatrically disturbed boys.' *Journal of Psychological Medicine,* **4,** 4-18.

Sheridan, M. D. (1969) 'The development of vision, hearing and communication in babies and young children.' *Proceedings of the Royal Society of Medicine,* **62,** 999-1004.

Steinhausen, H. Chr. (1976) 'Das hyperkinetische Syndrom.' *Klinische Pädiatrie,* **188,** 396-407.

Stemmer, C. (1964) *Choreiforme Bewegingsonrust (een Orienterend Onderzoek).* Thesis, Groningen.

Stephenson, P. S. (1975) 'The hyperkinetic syndrome: some misleading assumptions.' *Canadian Medical Association Journal,* **113,** 764, 767-769.

Stine, O. C., Saratsiotis, J. B., Masser, R. S. (1975) Relationships between neurological findings and classroom behavior.' *American Journal of Diseases of Children,* **129,** 1036-1040.

Strauss, A. A., Werner, H. (1943) 'Comparative psychopathology of the brain-injured child and the traumatic brain-injured adult.' *American Journal of Psychiatry,* **99,** 835-838.

Tardieu, G. (1968) 'L'infirmité motrice cérébrale. Etude critique des termes couramment utilisés.' *Revue de Neuropsychiatrie Infantile,* **16,** 1-5.

—— (1968) 'Le dossier clinique de l'infirmité motrice cérébrale. Méthodes d'évaluation et applications therapeutiques.' *Revue de Neuropsychiatrie Infantile,* **16,** 6-90.

Touwen, B. C. L. (1972) 'Laterality and dominance.' *Developmental Medicine and Child Neurology,* **14,** 747-758.

—— (1974) 'Neurological development of the infant.' *in* Davis, J. A., Dobbing, J. (Eds.) *Scientific Foundations of Paediatrics.* London: Heinemann. pp. 615-625.

—— (1976) *Neurological Development in Infancy. Clinics in Developmental Medicine, No. 58.* London: S.I.M.P. with Heinemann.

—— (1978*a*) 'Minimal brain dysfunction and minor neurological dysfunction.' *Advances in Biological Psychiatry,* **1,** 55-67.

—— (1978*b*) 'Variability and stereotypy in normal and deviant development.' *in* Apley, J. (Ed.) *Care of the Handicapped Child. Clinics in Developmental Medicine, No. 67.* London: S.I.M.P. with Heinemann Medical. pp. 99-110.

—— (1979) 'Laterality.' *in* Rutter, M. (Ed.) *Scientific Foundations of Developmental Psychiatry.* London: Heinemann Medical.

Walton, J. N. (1963) 'Clumsy children.' *in* Bax, M., Mac Keith, R. (Eds.) *Minimal Cerebral Dysfunction. Clinics in Developmental Medicine, No. 10.* London: Spastics Society with Heinemann. pp. 24-25.

Walzer, S., Richmond, J. B. (1973) 'The epidemiology of learning disorders.' *Pediatric Clinics of North America,* **20,** 549-565.

—— Wolff, P. H. (Eds.) (1973) 'Minimal cerebral dysfunction in children.' *Seminars in Psychiatry,* **5,** (1).

Wender, P. H. (1971) *Minimal Brain Dysfunction in Children.* New York: John Wiley.

Werry, J. S. (1968) 'Studies on the hyperactive child. IV. An empirical analysis of the minimal brain dysfunction syndrome.' *Archives of General Psychiatry,* **19,** 9-16.

Wolff, P. H., Hurwitz, I. (1966) 'The choreiform syndrome.' *Developmental Medicine and Child Neurology,* **8,** 160-165.
—— —— (1973) 'Functional implications of the minimal brain damage syndrome.' *Seminars in Psychiatry,* **5,** 105-115.
Yule, W. (1978) 'Developmental psychological assessment.' *Advances in Biological Psychiatry,* **1,** 35-54.
Zazzo, R. (Ed.) *Manuel pour l'Examination Psychologique de l'Enfant.* Neuchâtel: de la Chaux et Niestlé.

ACKNOWLEDGEMENTS

I thank Professor Heinz Prechtl for his great help and stimulating discussion during the writing of large parts of this book.

This work was supported by a grant from Prinses Beatrix Fonds and the Organisation for Health Research T.N.O.